URI GELLER'S MINDPOWER KIT

Uri Geller

PENGUIN STUDIO

PENGUIN STUDIO
Published by the Penguin Group
Penguin Books USA Inc., 375 Hudson Street,
New York, New York 10014, U.S.A.
Penguin Books Ltd, 27 Wrights Lane,
London W8 5TZ, England
Penguin Books Australia Ltd, Ringwood,
Victoria, Australia
Penguin Books Canada Ltd, 10 Alcorn Avenue,
Toronto, Ontario, Canada M4V 3B2
Penguin Books (N.Z.) Ltd, 182–190 Wairau Road,
Auckland 10, New Zealand

Penguin Books Ltd, Registered Offices:
Harmondsworth, Middlesex, England

First American edition
Published in 1996 by Penguin Studio,
an imprint of Penguin Books USA Inc.

1 3 5 7 9 10 8 6 4 2

A NOTE TO THE READER:
If you have a health problem, please consult your physician before
attempting any of the healing techniques and exercises described in this
kit. The publisher cannot accept responsibility for any mishaps or
accidents arising from the use of the items in the kit or arising out of
the techniques described herein. The audiocassette is a deeply relaxing
experience; under no circumstances should it be played while driving or
operating machinery or doing anything that requires your full attention.

CIP data available.
ISBN 0-670-87138-9

Printed in U.S.A.
Set in Goudy
Designed by Michael Mendelsohn at MM Design 2000, Inc.

ACKNOWLEDGMENTS

I would like to thank my family, my close friends,
and all my associates and colleagues around the world
for their encouragement and support throughout my life.

•

I owe special thanks to Marie Timell for her tremendous effort in
helping me with the American edition of this book. I would also
like to thank Jane Struthers for her editorial assistance with the
original British version of *The Mindpower Kit*.

~~~ CONTENTS ~~~

FOREWORD

~~~~~

I was delighted to be asked to write the foreword to *Uri Geller's Mindpower Kit*. In all the years I have known Uri—and we first met in the early 1970s—I have been fascinated by his astonishing powers and the way they have excited the imagination of people the world over. Recently we worked together on television again, and I was thrilled by the way a whole new generation of viewers responded to Uri's extraordinary psychic talents.

However, Uri does not aspire to be an exclusionary icon—his is an enabling talent. He wants to share what he has developed with as many people as he can. He wants to help others to achieve part, at least, of what he has achieved. So, if you have always been interested in your psychic potential and want to know more about how to tap into what Uri calls our sixth sense, this kit is an ideal starting point.

Sir David Frost, O.B.E.

INTRODUCTION

〜〜〜

I am no stranger to controversy. It has surrounded me ever since I was a kid growing up in Tel Aviv, so I've learned to live with it. I've even gotten used to reading stories about myself in newspapers and magazines that owe more to fiction than to accurate reporting. I still find it surprising when I read stories that are actually true. Maybe that's because they are fairly rare.

I often wonder which stories the public believes. Some of the things that have happened to me are described in this book and really are extraordinary. But as you read about them, I want you to bear this in mind—there's no reason why they shouldn't happen to you, too. In fact, I want them to happen to you. Let me tell you why.

Our minds are capable of remarkable, incredible feats, yet we don't use them to their full capacity. In fact, most of us use only about 10 percent of our brains, if that. The other 90 percent is full of untapped potential and undiscovered abilities. Our minds are operating in a limited way instead of at total capacity.

I believe that we once had full power over our minds, but that as our world has become more sophisticated and complex we have forgotten many of the abilities we once had. Abilities like telepathy, levitation, and being completely in tune with our bodies have all taken a backseat while other human abilities have been emphasized and developed. During the past hundred years, our incredible powers of invention have been on the rise, with the results being airplanes, space flight, computers, television, the movies, and all the other wonderful things we now take for granted. Very few people believed these inventions possible, yet now we don't find anything unusual about them. Like the ability to invent, I hope the same revolutionary expansion of capacity will take place with other unused areas of the mind.

We still have abilities like telepathy, although some people have forgotten how to use them. It's been different for me. For some reason, my psychic powers started working when I was a child, and they have been with me ever since. This kit has been designed to help you tune into your own mindpower, but before I describe all the fantastic things you can teach yourself to do, I want to tell you a little about my life so that you know a few of the astonishing things the human mind is capable of. I call it human potential.

How It All Started

I began my career as an entertainer in Israel, where I had a stage act that included reading the minds of people in the audience, bending spoons, rings, and bracelets, and starting broken watches. I was doing okay, although many people thought my powers were due to sleight of hand.

My stage act wasn't really any different from the things I did in my private life. I had grown up with my psychic powers, so although I found them astonishing—and still do—they weren't something I had invented just to make a name for myself. As far as I can remember, my powers were activated after two strange experiences as a child. The first happened when I was about four. I used to play in a deserted garden near my home in Tel Aviv. I loved that garden; it was my private domain. Late one afternoon I was playing there as usual when I heard a peculiar, high-pitched ringing in my ears. I'd never heard anything like it before. It felt as if time had stopped, and when I looked up, the sun and blue sky had vanished. In their place was a strong, silvery light that was moving toward me. It moved nearer and nearer until I passed out. When I woke up, I was lying on the grass, unharmed. I ran home to tell my mother, who reacted in the classic way of all mothers when they're worried—she got angry with me.

The second weird event, which may or may not have helped to trigger my psychic powers, involved electricity. My mother worked as a seamstress to make extra money, and one day, as she was working, I noticed a bright blue light coming out of her sewing machine. I'd never seen anything like it, so I went over and stuck my fingers in the light. The shock hurled me three or four feet into the air, and I landed on the floor. You don't have to be psychic to know how my poor mother reacted.

It was around this time, when I was about five or six, that I began to realize there was something extraordinary going on. I didn't know what to make of the peculiar things that kept happening. For instance, my parents had given me a watch that I was very proud of, so I was really upset when it started acting up and running fast. I have to admit that I didn't enjoy school at all and used to long for the final class to be over, so you can imagine my disappointment when I would look at my watch and see that it was time to go home, then glance up at the wall clock and find that the class was only half over after all. Each time, I would reset my watch and grit my teeth as the minutes slowly dragged past. I told my mother there was something wrong with my watch, and I left it at home with her so she could see for herself. But nothing happened and it behaved perfectly. Until I put it back on my wrist, that is; then it started all its old tricks again. A watch is a rather delicate instrument, and I believe that I activated it without my conscious awareness. This may have been because, subconsciously, I wanted time to pass quickly in school. That's why my mind was triggering these energies to move the watch's hands.

Finally, my parents bought me another watch. At last, I thought, I've got a decent watch. On the first day I wore it, I looked down to check the time and saw that the hands had curled up as if they were trying to break out of the glass casing. I didn't wear a watch for a long time after that, and I still don't generally wear one.

I had already discovered that I could bend spoons when I was four. Rather inconveniently, I was having my lunch at the time. My mother had made me mushroom soup, and I was eating it at the kitchen table when the soup spoon just seemed to sag in the middle and its bowl fell off, depositing hot soup in my lap. My mother and I couldn't make any sense of it.

As I grew older, I started to put two and two together. I knew that something strange was happening to me, and that it obviously didn't happen to other people. All the strange events were leading me to believe that my thoughts alone could move matter. Weird things would happen at inconvenient or embarrassing moments, which made me feel awkward, mortified, and very isolated. Yet when I tried to show off my powers, such as making the hands of a watch move, my school friends laughed or thought I was playing a trick on them. This made me feel uncomfortable, like an oddball.

INTRODUCTION

My parents even suggested that I see a psychiatrist to get it all straightened out. As I grew up, I learned not to talk about what happened to me, because I knew it singled me out from everyone else.

Later, however, after I fulfilled my required national service in the Israeli army in 1968, I started working as an entertainer. I enjoyed being on stage and using my powers. Gradually, word spread about me. For example, when a reporter asked Prime Minister Golda Meir what she could predict for Israel in the coming year, she replied, "Why don't you ask Uri Geller?"

In the summer of 1971, a scientist named Andrija Puharich visited me in Tel Aviv. He had heard about me and wanted to find out for himself whether what I did was real. Andrija soon decided that I was on the level and persuaded me that I should let the scientific community prove that my powers were genuine, and therefore worth further investigation, by undergoing a whole range of experiments under strictly controlled conditions.

In the spring of 1972 I went to Germany to do some public appearances. The press there first trumpeted that I was a magician, not a psychic, but then the headlines went wild when I was able to stop a cable car in midair and managed to make an escalator grind to a halt, all through psychokinesis (see page 125). While in Germany, I decided to take Puharich's advice and permit my powers to be scientifically tested. I was investigated by Dr. Friedbert Karger of the renowned Max Planck Institute of Plasma Physics. In one experiment Dr. Karger held a metal ring. When I touched it briefly, it twisted so badly out of shape that it cracked in two places. The scientists at the institute examined that ring in minute detail and concluded that the markings of the metal stress looked the same as

6

INTRODUCTION

if a pair of pliers had been used to twist the ring. I hadn't used any
sort of tool. The institute announced, "The powers of this man are
a phenomenon that theoretical physics cannot explain." It was the
beginning of my participation in many scientific experiments.

From Germany, I went to California and began what turned
out to be a long and extensive series of experiments at Stanford Research Institute, now called SRI International. The experiments
were conducted by scientists from several countries, under the di-
rectorship of two laser physicists, Dr. Hal Puthoff and Russell Targ.
Andrija Puharich was involved, as was Captain Edgar Mitchell,
who was the sixth man on the moon as part of the Apollo 14 mission, and who became one of my good friends.

They almost turned me inside out at SRI, trying to discover
what I do and how I do it. The scientists began by studying the
things I did as an entertainer, such as telepathy and spoon bending,
and then went on to tests that they devised—for example, asking
me to erase the images on videotapes or influence an electric scale
on which was placed a gram weight. The scale was isolated under a
glass bell jar. The scale showed that the gram weight sometimes
weighed more and sometimes less. During these experiments I
would sit quietly, focusing on the object in question, and concentrate all my mental energy on it, at the same time focusing on a
suitable message such as "Erase, erase" for the videotape or "Enlarge, enlarge" when I wanted the gram weight to become heavier.

While I was fascinated by what I was undergoing at SRI, it was
an unnerving experience to sit still and concentrate for so long. It
was not made any easier by the fact that my powers had started to
attract some odd phenomena: Objects would levitate; others would
vanish into thin air in front of the bemused gaze of myself and

INTRODUCTION

whoever else was present; cassette tape recorders would pick up messages for me from disembodied mechanical voices; cassettes inside the tape recorder would be there one minute and would vanish the next; and the play button of the cassette player sometimes switched itself on.

Then, the weirdest experience of all happened one November evening in New York.

I was staying in an apartment on the East Side and had been visiting my friends Byron and Maria Janis, who also lived on the East Side. I left their apartment at 5:30 P.M. to buy a present at Bloomingdale's before going home to shower and change, then to meet a friend at 6:30 P.M. Bloomingdale's was jammed with shoppers, so I bought what I wanted in a nearby store, then started home. Just after 6:00, I began jogging because I didn't want to be late. Suddenly I had the oddest sensation, almost as if I were running backward, and I felt my body shoot upward. The next thing I saw was a porch screen, and I realized I was in the air, hurtling toward it. Luckily, I had time to brace myself for the impact, then *whoosh*, I shot through the screen and landed on a glass-topped table, inside a house. I slid across the table and landed on the floor with a crash, toppling the table. I was really shocked—and not only because I had apparently flown through the air. I was also shocked because I recognized my surroundings: I was in Andrija's Puharich house in Ossining, thirty miles north of New York.

At 6:15 P.M. that evening, Andrija was watching television when he heard a terrible splintering of glass and came to investigate. He couldn't believe his eyes when he saw me lying on the floor amid the ruins of his table. I was pretty freaked out myself. While I was still recovering, Maria coincidentally rang Andrija from New

York. When Andrija handed me the phone so I could talk to her, Maria was almost speechless with amazement. I had left her apartment only forty-five or fifty minutes earlier. There was no way I could have gotten to Ossining in that time by ordinary means.

The SRI released its findings from the tests on me in March 1973 at a meeting sponsored by the Columbia University Department of Physics: "As a result of Geller's success in this experimental period, we consider that he has demonstrated his paranormal perceptual ability in a convincing and unambiguous manner." They stated that they had no explanation for the phenomena they had witnessed under controlled conditions, so they wanted to conduct further tests.

I was delighted that the SRI tests showed what I had known all along—that the unusual things I am able to do are the result of my mindpower alone and have nothing to do with clever conjuring tricks or distracting the observer. I have been accused of utilizing a variety of weird techniques to achieve what I do, from having a laser beam concealed up my sleeve (do you honestly think I'd have any arms left by this time if such a thing were true?), to daubing metal-bending chemicals on my hands (what state would my fingers be in by now?), to hypnotizing my observers or having radio transmitters embedded in my teeth.

As we were nearing the end of the tests, we heard that *Time* magazine was planning to publish a damning account of them, regardless of the facts. They wanted advance copies of the SRI report, which wasn't possible; Hal Puthoff and Russell Targ were planning to publish their findings in the prestigious scientific journal *Nature*, which they duly did in the October 18, 1974, issue. It was like unleashing a dam—we were hit by a tidal wave of negative reporting. The *New Scientist* magazine covered *Nature's* story and invited a panel of experts to air their views. The magazine thoroughly trashed the SRI findings for being nonscientific yet did so in a nonscientific way itself. And it's been like that ever since.

I firmly believe that everyone is entitled to express his or her own opinions, but what has never failed to amaze me is the way that some people are so eager to dismiss something simply because they don't understand it. Even some reputable scientists, who you might think would know better, refuse to entertain new ideas if they don't fit into their own theories. If something doesn't link up with their view of the world, they dismiss it out of hand as being impossible.

Psychic phenomena occur in many forms, some of which are described in this book. They include psychokinesis, dowsing, healing, clairaudience (the ability to hear things that are inaudible to others), and clairvoyance (the ability to see things that are invisible to others). All these phenomena harness our sixth sense, which is our psychic ability. Many people are psychic, yet they don't realize it because they dismiss what happens to them as coincidence or put it down to an overactive imagination. I believe that if more people tapped into their psychic powers, and understood that there are other realms than just our existence here on earth, mankind would benefit greatly. We would understand one another better, which would lead to fewer conflicts on a personal level and would help to bring about world peace.

As the 1970s drew to a close, I bowed out of the public spotlight for a while. There were things I had to sort out, including my

INTRODUCTION

health and my private life. I used my willpower to conquer the eating disorder bulimia, which was threatening my life. I married, and my wife, Hanna, and I had two wonderful children, Daniel and Natalie. I did confidential work for companies, private individuals, and certain government agencies, and I also developed a new career as a dowser for big mining and oil companies. In the mid-1980s, my family and I moved from America to Great Britain, to a small village near London, where we still live.

Using This Kit

The mindpower kit consists of this book, the energized crystal, empowered orange meditation circle, and cassette. It has been designed to help you tune into your own mental abilities, to trigger psychic powers you never knew you had, and to make the most of your mindpower. I ask you to read this book with an open mind. Think about what I have to say, and try some of the exercises described in the various chapters. When you read the chapter on willpower, you may discover that for the first time in your life you are able to stop smoking, cut down on your drinking, or lose weight and keep it off. If you are plagued by insomnia, the combination of this book and my tape could help you to reprogram your mind to allow you to get a good night's sleep again.

The hour-long cassette tape contains my special psyching-up session, which you can use whenever your willpower needs a boost. The rhythms and harmonies of the accompanying music have been created to inspire you and to help trigger your psychic powers. The second side of the tape contains specific exercises to boost your confidence, activate your healing powers, and help you quit smoking and beat stress, plus several other exercises. When you play the tape, listen carefully to my words. Sit quietly by yourself. Know that I am talking directly to you. Absorb the mantras or affirmations I have recorded for you. Concentrate on what I am saying. Look at the photograph of me on the front cover of the kit if you need assistance—it can help you trigger your willpower. You can play the tape whenever you need it, or you might prefer to play it once a week to stay in top mental form. Do not play it while driving or operating machinery.

When you concentrate on the orange circle that comes with this kit and that is designed to increase your willpower and your ability to concentrate, or if you place broken watches on it, you could be delighted by the positive results. Carrying the crystal could improve your health and increase your sense of optimism and introduce you to the amazing powers of crystals. You can even use the crystal to instruct them to start working again to heal.

While the kit may not turn you into another Uri Geller overnight, it will certainly help you develop your own psychic powers, use more of your brain, and generally enhance all aspects of your life. The only thing that's stopping you from opening up the frontiers of your brain is you. Everything else that you need is contained in this kit. So why not embark on a voyage of mental discovery, with me as your guide? It will change your life!

VISUALIZATION

~~~

When I was a child, I fantasized a lot, especially when I was supposed to be concentrating on my schoolwork. I would let my mind wander, and I would mentally vanish into a world of my own. I mostly thought about spaceships and exploring other galaxies, but I also dreamed about the things I longed for, such as a new toy, a puppy, a catapult. To my astonishment, the things that I dreamed about would soon enter my life. It seemed that one week I was thinking about how great it would be to have a new watch, and the following week I had one. This was particularly surprising because our family was not exactly rolling in money, so it was almost like a miracle for these things to appear. "How come," I would wonder, "I was just thinking about how great it would be to have a puppy, and I got one?" I know the answer now—I wasn't only thinking about these things, I was visualizing them. Visualizing is simply using your imagination to see something in your mind's eye. And it is visualization that can help you change your life.

My mother adored playing cards with her friends, and she taught me to play when I was a little kid. We discovered a strange thing—I always knew when she was holding the joker, even though I could see only the back of her cards. I would visualize the cards she was holding, and after lots of practice I was able to tell her exactly which card was the joker because I could "see" it.

13

VISUALIZATION

I began trying to help her win whenever she visited her card club. I knew what the club looked like because she had taken me there. When she went off to the club I would sit at home and visualize the room, picture my mother sitting at the card table with her friends, then visualize her being paid her winnings at the end of each game. I would wait impatiently for her to come home from the club so I could learn whether I had gotten my visualization right or not. She would come into my bedroom and sit on the bed beside me. "Well, Uri," she would ask, "how did I do tonight?" I would tell her what I had seen, and then, if I was right, she would smile delightedly and, with a flourish, produce the money from her handbag. I got it right more often than not. It was through her card-playing winnings that my mother was able to buy me the small things I dreamed of. Today, I believe I was both *predicting* that my mother would win and *helping* her to win with my mind's power.

When I was seven, I fell in love with games and sports. I loved running and playing Ping-Pong, but basketball was my big favorite. I would sit in the movie theater watching films of the top basketball players racing around the court and scoring goals, and I really envied them. Why couldn't I be that good? I knew the only way I could emulate them was to practice, practice, practice, which, I have to admit, didn't always appeal to me. Like most kids, I wanted instant results. And then I got them! I discovered that I could produce fantastic hook shots by concentrating on the ball. Just before throwing it, I would imagine it going straight into the basket. Then I would throw the ball and follow it with my eyes to guide it, using a mental force that I believe to be psychic.

Visualization is now a part of my life, and I use it every day. It's as natural to me as breathing. In fact, it's as automatic as that. I visualize business deals going well, I visualize broken appliances working again, I visualize my family staying healthy, I even visualize obtaining a parking space when I need one.

How to Visualize

As I grew older, I developed a system for my visualization. These days, I picture a television screen in my head and visualize a scene on it, but when we lived in Israel I had never seen a TV—I didn't even know what one looked like. But I was an avid moviegoer, so I used to picture a white-gray movie screen with a green rim. At first I had to close my eyes to see it, but then, I gradually got used to visualizing it while I had my eyes open and I was doing something else, such as playing with my friends, running, walking, or trying to concentrate on my schoolwork. Soon I was able to switch on this imaginary screen automatically and project my fantasy onto it.

There is nothing mysterious about visualization, although you may have to practice for a while until you feel confident about what you are doing. Just imagine you are looking at a TV screen in your mind. If you've never done this before you might find it difficult at first, so I suggest that you sit or stand near a TV screen, look at it close up, and shut your eyes tightly, screwing them up hard. That will imprint the image of the TV screen on your mind's eye. It's as if you have photocopied it onto your mind.

Visualization works best when you are feeling relaxed and at ease. The power of the unconscious mind is strongest then, and the positive images that we create make a bigger impact. As you get used to visualizing, you'll be able to do it quickly, in all sorts of conditions, but at first I would recommend that you choose a time when you know you won't be interrupted, and when you've got some time to yourself. Sit comfortably in a chair (if you lie down you may fall asleep!), close your eyes, and spend a couple of minutes relaxing. Now, you are ready to begin to visualize.

Next, project the images that you want onto that TV screen. Picture yourself pulling off a big business deal, being a success at an interview, feeling healthy again, having a safe journey home, or being able to touch your toes when you exercise. In other words, picture whatever you want to happen. Do it every day, see yourself being successful, and truly believe in what you are seeing. The positive results could really surprise you! By the way, if you have some astonishing experiences with visualization, I would love to hear them. Write to me at the address given on page 132.

How to Strengthen Inner Vision

Another exercise that I practice might sound strange, but I believe that if your eyes are in good shape, your inner vision is also in good shape. You should do this exercise to strengthen your eyes even if you wear glasses. I exercise my eyes every day, and I must be doing something right. Although I am nearly fifty, I don't need spectacles. (Please check with your doctor or optician first if you suffer from eye problems.) You may prefer to do this exercise when you're by yourself; it can look strange to onlookers.

Look straight in front of you. Then, without moving your head, look up, look down, look to the right, look to the left, roll your eyes to the right and to the left. You should feel the muscles in your eyes pulling, which means you are giving them a good workout. Try to perform the exercise as slowly as you can for maximum benefit. Now take a pencil and hold it about twelve inches from your nose. Look at it while you slowly move it toward you, until it touches your nose. Move it away from you again, still watching it. Something else you can do is move the pencil around and look at it from as many angles as possible, still without moving your head. If you do these exercises for a few minutes once a day, you will be astonished at the beneficial results.

The Importance of Self-Love

For visualization to be successful, you must be able to create a positive image in your mind's eye of yourself. This is impossible unless you feel self-love. Many people find the idea of making a point of loving yourself odd, embarrassing, or indulgent. That's because they get it confused with the idea of being in love with yourself, with being obsessed with yourself, with believing that you are the only important person on the planet. But that is an extreme of what I am talking about, which is learning to be kind to yourself, to appreciate your talents and gifts, to respect yourself, and to learn how to protect yourself against people, emotions, and situations that do you harm or drain you of energy. If these ideas are unfamiliar to you, it will take some time for you to get used to them, but gradually you will become better able to put them into practice and will learn to have more faith in yourself.

Learning to love yourself can be very complicated. It has such a lot to do with your upbringing. During your childhood you learn the customs, traits, mannerisms, speech patterns, feelings, and tendencies of your parents, and throughout your life it is as if you have an umbilical cord attached to your childhood. Even when you were a fetus in your mother's womb you would have tuned in to the emotional atmosphere that surrounded you. If you were brought up in a happy, loving family you have a head start when it comes to loving yourself; with luck, you will already have learned to appreciate yourself. But if you were raised in a family in which feelings were never shown, physical displays of affection such as hugs and good-night kisses were frowned upon, and everything you did was criticized, or in which one parent was emotionally distant or physically absent, you will find it much harder.

I believe that if you can learn to love yourself, you will automatically protect yourself from the worst of your worries. When things aren't going well we worry about our health, our work, and our relationships, and that starts to affect us badly. Unless you learn to take life in stride, you can be exhausted by worry—you can't sleep properly, you feel listless and out of sorts, everything seems a big effort, and you can't enjoy yourself. Worrying uses up a lot of valuable energy, which is why so many people lose weight or become ill when they are seriously concerned about something. You are transferring your vital energy away from yourself and your well-being to whatever is worrying you.

There are two aspects to loving yourself—loving the inner you, and loving the outer you. I think it is more important to love the inner you, but you mustn't neglect taking care of your outer self. That is the first thing people see when they meet you. Most people judge others by their appearance, even though the outer image may not reflect who the real person is inside. Virtually the whole world is built on that, so it is important for you to look good. By loving yourself you will create an inner glow, and you will want to take care of yourself. Healthy habits, proper hygiene, and neatness go a long way in creating a good impression. You don't have to spend a fortune to look great, but you do have to love yourself. You can transform your looks if you take care of yourself, wear flattering clothes in colors that suit you, have a good haircut, and keep your body in shape. After all, part of loving yourself is simply taking time for yourself and spending it on looking good.

Mirroring for Self Love

There are several techniques for learning to love and positively reinforce yourself. The primary way is called mirroring yourself, which means learning to talk to yourself. Gaze into your own eyes, look into your black pupils, and mentally allow yourself to go deep into them. I believe that this will help you dissolve the everyday barriers between you and other people. Although we are all individuals, my view is that we were all created by one God—no matter what our religion is—and that on a deep, spiritual level we are all equal and are part of one another. It is as if we are all brothers and sisters, we are all part of God's family, and we all belong together. Once you are at one with everything, you will feel a wonderful sense of peace and understanding. Suddenly your comprehension of life will deepen; and you will sense that oneness every time you stare into your eyes in the mirror. Tap into those loving feelings and give them to yourself. Tell yourself that you are always fine, always taken care of, always safe. Remind yourself that you are part of God's family and that you are at peace.

VISUALIZATION

Next focus on your outer self (stand in front of a full-length mirror if you wish). First of all, you can assess your appearance. Stand naked in front of a full-length mirror and examine yourself. If you are objective, you will see what others see when they look at you. I think it is very important to be aware of your pluses and minuses. Look hard, and decide what you can change to improve your appearance and what you must learn to live with. There's not a lot you can do if you've got very wide feet and wish they were dainty and narrow (although you can choose shoes and boots that make your feet look slimmer), but you *can* change a pair of glasses that don't suit you and you can lose that ugly spare tire around your waist. If there is something you wish to change, don't be hard on yourself. Loving yourself means staying positive. Tell yourself, "Because I love myself, I'm going to do myself the favor of getting a great new haircut" or "Because I love myself, I'm going to walk to work every day." Look, too, for the parts of you that you wouldn't change, such as your lovely eyes or beautiful hair. Tell yourself: "I like what I see."

You can also use the mirror to boost your self-confidence. Stand in front of it and look deep into your eyes, then tell yourself that you're successful, that you're popular, that people love you, and that as you grow older you're becoming wiser and more experienced. Repeat an affirmation out loud while looking in the mirror.

In the chapter on willpower I describe how to use mirroring to slow down the aging process, and you can use the other techniques in this chapter in the same way.

VISUALIZATION

Visualization and Your Health

I believe that visualization has many health benefits. You may find this idea quite controversial or peculiar at first, but I ask you to keep an open mind and then, if you want, to try it for yourself. After all, what have you got to lose?

Have you ever dreaded having to do something, such as visit some difficult relatives or see your accountant, only to find that you don't have to go after all because you develop a serious cold or a violent stomach bug at the last minute? Most of us would probably say yes. Have you ever read about a particular disease in a medical encyclopedia and then felt seriously alarmed because you had apparently developed its symptoms the following day? Yes? I think these situations happen because our minds are so sophisticated and powerful. All that is needed is the tiniest of suggestions for our minds to affect our bodies. In other words, we can think ourselves ill, whether we are consciously aware of it or not.

To many people, that is an astonishing thought. But if that is astonishing, then how about being able to think ourselves well? You can actually use the power of your mind, through visualization, to heal yourself, control pain, and keep yourself healthy.

In this section, I am going to show you how to use visualization to make yourself fitter and healthier. Before I describe my techniques, I want to impress on you that you should always have health problems checked out by a doctor first. Don't take any risks with your health—it's not worth it. If the doctor diagnoses a particular problem and treats it, you can use these visualization techniques in conjunction with the treatment.

VISUALIZATION

Illness as a Symptom of Other Problems

A very important part of controlling illness is discovering how you became ill in the first place, and the cause may not always be as obvious as you think. Let's pretend that every now and then you wake up with a deep sense of foreboding, a thundering headache, and brief but unpleasant stomach upset. It seems to be happening a lot, and you begin to worry. Is this the start of some sinister disease? You see your doctor, who can find nothing wrong. Then, when you think about it, you realize that it always seems to happen on Sunday mornings, but only alternate Sundays. In fact, you think, it's odd, because the upset stomach always strikes on the Sundays that your parents are coming to brunch. That's when you will have to race around all morning doing the cooking, ask your children to tidy their rooms, and remind your partner not to discuss politics with your parents because it always ends in a big fight. Is this a coincidence? I don't think so. No wonder you feel ill! Your symptoms are perfectly genuine, but they have a psychological rather than a physical cause. You've got to do something about your parents' visits, and then your stomach problems will go away! And if your stomach turns over at the very thought of standing up for yourself, you need to bolster your self-confidence by learning to love and respect yourself, exactly in the ways described on pages 18–19.

All sorts of minor ailments can be alleviated once you discover what's setting them off. For instance, maybe you always get indigestion after dinner, which you eat sitting on the sofa in front of the TV set. Perhaps you're sitting in a way that makes it difficult for your digestive processes to work properly, or perhaps when you're eating you stare at the TV screen but don't notice what's on it because your mind is busy replaying the day's events, dwelling on the

VISUALIZATION

way your new colleague is driving you crazy, or the fact that you've got far too much work to do and you don't know how to cope. If you think about it, no wonder you suffer from indigestion! The first problem has a practical solution—eat at a table, or, on the sofa, put lots of cushions behind your back so that you sit up straight—but what about the other problems?

This is where self-love comes in again. What you must do is find a way to stop the problems from ruining your life—and your digestion. Taking an antacid probably won't help one bit, because the problems will still be there even if your indigestion isn't. Maybe you need to talk to your colleague, as diplomatically as possible, about how he or she is disturbing you. He or she may not even be aware of the effect he or she is having on you unless you say something. A lot of people would rather put up with all kinds of abuse and hassle rather than take a deep breath and talk to someone, yet it can have miraculous results. Even if you can't solve your problems overnight by taking that first step toward improving your life—by talking about them—you will feel so much better because you'll be doing something positive.

But what do you do if you can't shut off your worries each night? I think the answer lies in visualization. What you must do is imagine those problems as a physical object—perhaps a lot of heavy stones, or a dead weight, or a lump of lead—and then picture yourself locking them in a room. Say to yourself that you know they are in there and that you can unlock the door if you want to look at them, but in the meantime you are going to stop thinking about them and do something enjoyable instead. Every time your mind strays back to them, say to yourself, "Stop!" Visualize yourself turning your back on that room and walking away from it.

23

EASING A TENSION HEADACHE

Look straight in front of you while moving your shoulders around in a circle. Keeping your head still, hunch your shoulders up toward your ears, move them back, down, forward, and back up toward your ears again. Do this in a slow, smooth, movement, and imagine the muscles in your neck and shoulders losing their tension. If you like, you could picture them as a tangled skein of wool, and as you move your shoulders around you can visualize that wool starting to unknot itself until eventually it is looking beautifully smooth again. Massage the back of your neck, kneading the tense muscles with your fingertips. Work up and down your neck, and as you do so imagine those muscles relaxing and the blood flowing properly again. Finish by massaging your temples in a circular motion.

If you are worrying about things you are completely unable to change, or about something that happened in the past, maybe you should get rid of those worries once and for all. Perhaps you should imagine the worries turning into clouds or feathers, and picture them drifting up into the sky and dispersing. Tell yourself that the worries have now vanished and you are going to get on with the rest of your life. If your mind strays back to them, picture those clouds or feathers again and tell yourself firmly that your worries have now gone. You will soon forget all about them.

USING VISUALIZATION TO COMBAT MINOR HEALTH PROBLEMS

Before I start talking about ways to combat minor health problems, I want to mention a technique that ensures you stay healthy. After all, if you believe, as I do, that our thoughts can make us ill, then we can also use our thoughts to keep well. As discussed earlier, this exercise is very simple, but it works. Make the saying or affirmation containing a positive message that you repeat to yourself a couple of times every day specific to your health. It is especially good to do this when you are mirroring yourself. You can make up your own, but here is a good one to begin with: "Today is the beginning of the rest of my life." You can change the affirmation according to your circumstances, but always make sure that it stays positive, and always believe 100 percent in what you are saying.

Here are some positive health affirmations that you can repeat to yourself whenever you need to, to keep yourself healthy or to think yourself well. As you repeat them to yourself, truly believe in what you are saying. Know that what you are saying will make you healthier.

~ My body is completely healthy.
~ I am in perfect health. I feel great!
~ Every day, I become healthier and happier.
~ My headache [or whatever is wrong] is going away.
~ My immune system is working perfectly.

GUIDELINES FOR HEALING MINOR HEALTH PROBLEMS

- Always consult your doctor about any health problems that are worrying you.
- Create a mantra or positive affirmation that will help you keep healthy, and repeat it every day.
- Accept that the state of your mind can affect your well-being.
- Conjure up a mental picture of your ailment, then imagine its being soothed away or vanishing into thin air.
- Train yourself to take several short breaks each day, during which you completely relax your body and mind.

~~~~~

Using visualization for minor health problems is quite simple, and you can develop any technique you wish for your particular complaint. For example, let's start off with a technique for helping indigestion, which is something that plagues many people. Next time you get indigestion or heartburn, imagine that your stomach is being flooded with a very soothing, milky liquid. Feel how silky the liquid is, and picture it gently reducing the amount of acid in your stomach. If it helps, imagine that the soothing liquid is white and the acid is a sharp lemon-yellow, then picture the color of the lemon-yellow liquid getting fainter and fainter until it fades into white. Concentrate hard on what you are imagining, and keep bringing your mind back to the visualization every time it drifts off into other distractions. Don't worry, if you've never done anything like this before; you'll soon get the hang of it. Soon you'll be able to control your indigestion and ease it without having to reach for any antacid remedies.

THE BENEFITS OF LAUGHTER

Finally, don't forget the benefits of laughter. Next time you're unwell, instead of thinking how miserable or ill you feel, watch a favorite film or comedy show or read a book that makes you laugh out loud. You'll soon start to perk up, but why? Believe it or not, your facial muscles are continually sending messages to your brain about what's going on around you. If you scowl or grind your teeth, your brain thinks that you are facing an emergency and produces lots of stress hormones and adrenaline to help you combat the problem. That's great if you're about to enter a fight or are about to have to run for your life, but if all you're doing is sitting at your desk

VISUALIZATION

What about headaches? Most headaches will cure themselves, given time, because they are caused by minor problems, but always seek medical advice if you are worried. There are several ways to help common headaches, and one of the simplest is to massage the part of your head that hurts. Gently rub it with the palm of your hand, and as you do so imagine that the pain is a jagged red line. Picture it on that TV screen in your head that I talked about earlier in the chapter (see pages 14–15), and watch the red line gradually

frowning at what's in front of you or fuming while you're stuck in a traffic jam, those hormones will stay in your bloodstream and make you feel even more tense and irritable. If this happens a lot, the hormones may eventually make you ill. On the other hand, the moment you smile or laugh, your brain releases chemicals, called endorphins, which are the body's natural tranquilizers. You relax, you feel good, and life seems worth living again. If you don't believe me, test it out for yourself right now. Scowl hard, and notice the effect it has on your body. Then smile, and you'll see how much better you suddenly feel.

fading from red to pink to almond and then to nothing. Breathe deeply and evenly. Feel the tension draining out of your body. Say to yourself, "I am making my headache go away. I am making my headache go away." Above all, believe in what you are doing.

You can use the same sort of technique for other minor ailments, by visualizing the injured or painful part of your body getting better. For instance, let's say that you burn your hand while taking something out of the oven. It's not a bad enough burn to need medical treatment, but it still needs attention. One good way to treat it is to run cold water over the burn for five minutes, then either cover it with a clean dressing or leave it uncovered. It will still hurt, which is where your visualization techniques come in. Visualize the burn as a large, bright red area of skin that is smarting and stinging. You probably won't need to use much imagination to do this! Now picture yourself stroking a soothing lotion on the area. Feel the welcome coolness of the liquid as it touches your skin, and picture yourself gently patting the lotion into your damaged skin. Feel it soothing your skin and starting to take the pain away. Concentrate very hard, because the technique won't work unless you really believe in it. After the liquid has soaked into your skin, picture the reddened skin starting to change color. Watch it slowly fade from an angry red until it is once again the color of your normal skin. Tell yourself that your burn is already starting to get better. Do this as often as you need to, until the pain has gone. Your burn will heal much faster than usual, although you will still have to treat it carefully, of course. Incidentally, you can still practice this visualization even if you do have to seek medical treatment.

There are visualization techniques for every ailment. If you are unlucky enough to break a bone, picture the jagged edges knitting

VISUALIZATION

together; if you strain a muscle, imagine the inflammation gradually lessening; if you cut yourself, visualize the two edges of the wound knitting together. Of course, you should always seek medical help if the injury is serious, which I strongly urge you to do. But these techniques can help your recovery and cause you to heal more quickly.

VISUALIZATION FOR SERIOUS ILLNESSES

I am now going to give you an exercise that can help when something much more serious is wrong. Cancer is one of the most feared diseases of all, and many cancer sufferers feel they personally have no control over their illness. However, I don't agree. Cancer sufferers can fight back by triggering their bodies to attack the cancer cells and stop them from spreading. Healers have been recommending techniques that enable one to do this for years. Scientists are testing the healers' techniques and are discovering that they really do have a positive physical effect on the body, as exhibited by an increased number of leukocytes, or white blood cells (which help fight infection), in the bloodstream.

Let me give you an example. Imagine a big fight going on in your bloodstream between the cancer cells and the white blood cells. You've got to make the white blood cells win. You might want to imagine that the cancer cells look like snarling wild animals, while the white blood cells look like spacemen with futuristic weapons. Select a time to do this when you won't be interrupted, make yourself comfortable, close your eyes, and picture that TV screen in your head. Start to imagine a huge battle going on between the bad guys (the cancer cells) and the good guys (the white blood cells). Picture a bad guy fighting with a good guy, then see the bad guy being killed or, even better, vaporized. Tell yourself that you have wiped out some cancer cells, and really believe it. You can also use this exercise if you have been laid low with a bad cold, flu, or mystery virus, or if you're suffering from any other disease that has gotten into your bloodstream. Keep at it, and do it several times a day if possible. It certainly can't hurt you, and it could save your life.

HOW TO CONTROL PAIN

Hundreds of millions of dollars are spent each year on pain remedies for just about every condition you can think of. Have a look in your bathroom cabinet or first-aid kit, and count how many bottles and packets of painkillers you can see. You probably reach for one of them whenever you need it, but have you ever wondered whether you yourself can make the pain go away?

We have all heard stories of actors and dancers who suffer some terrible injury in the wings but rise above the pain and continue with their performance. You've probably helped someone to rise above pain, especially if you have children. Imagine a little boy running happily across a back garden, clutching his favorite toy. Suddenly he stumbles and falls. His mother rushes over to him to check that he is all right, and she can see at a glance that he is slightly shocked and has lightly grazed his knee. The little boy's mouth quivers for a while, and then he starts to cry, saying his knee hurts. And what does his mother do? She kisses his knee better, gives him a hug, and lets him run off again, comforted and already

VISUALIZATION

having forgotten about his injury. Touching someone gently and placing your hands on him or her can diminish pain considerably. A verbal assurance and telepathic message to a child can result in a dramatic reduction in pain.

Let me give you another example. Imagine you are sitting in your doctor's office while she prepares the vaccination you need before you go on vacation to a country you've always wanted to visit. Anxiously, you watch her fill the syringe and then advance toward you, smiling. You try to smile back, but you are nervous and your top lip sticks to your teeth. You swallow hard. "This won't hurt," she says, as she swabs your arm with alcohol before inserting the needle, and you relax slightly. You look the other way and prepare yourself. You feel the needle go in and it *does* hurt, but what do you do? Unless you are a complete masochist or fascinated by needles, you immediately force yourself to stop thinking about the pain in your arm and focus instead on the poster on the opposite wall, or wonder what to have for lunch. Or, if you are smart, you think about what a wonderful time you are going to have on your vacation. You picture yourself lying on the beach, and you imagine the crashing of the waves on the shore until you can almost smell the suntan lotion you will be wearing. You may still be aware of the discomfort in your arm, but it will now feel quite remote.

Those are two examples of how to control pain, and they both involve distracting yourself. So the next time you are sitting in the dentist's chair or having a checkup, distance yourself from what is going on by visualizing yourself doing something wonderful. Maybe you see yourself sitting in a lovely garden, surrounded by sweet-smelling flowers and listening to the drone of bees, or perhaps you are at a concert given by your favorite singer. Whatever you imag-

VISUALIZATION

ine, as long as it is enjoyable, I can assure you that the dental or hospital appointment will be much more bearable than it would otherwise have been. Try it next time and see. Visualization distracts the mind and lessens pain. It works!

Using Visualization for Relaxation

Learning to relax is one of the keys to a happier, healthier life. Many ailments and diseases are caused by an inability to relax, and doctors now accept that stress can be a killer. Our modern lives are so busy, and so full of noise and bustle, that it can be difficult for us to find time to relax during the day. The only time we may find to do so is when we collapse into bed at night, and then we may be exhausted, tense, and unable to sleep. Instead, our minds buzz away, processing and going over everything that's happened during the day. Finally, we fall into a restless, broken sleep, only to wake up the following day feeling tired and jaded, and so the cycle continues.

I think the key to relaxation is to distract your mind from its everyday worries and to concentrate on something pleasant or enjoyable instead. One good way to relax is to set aside a few minutes when you can be by yourself, taking the phone off the hook if necessary. Then sit in a comfortable chair, with both feet on the floor and your hands resting gently in your lap. Close your eyes and breathe deeply several times. Each time you exhale, tell yourself that your whole body is relaxing. Feel your muscles relaxing, feel the tension draining away. Imagine that you're looking at a TV screen in your mind, just as you did for the visualization exercise. Picture a wonderful scene on the screen, such as a warm, sandy beach or some beautiful, snow-covered mountains. Imagine that you can hear the sounds of that scene, whether they're waves crashing on the shore or the joyous notes of birdsong. Smell the salt air or the delicate wildflowers. Really immerse yourself in that scene, and imagine that you're there. Enjoy it for a few minutes, then picture yourself walking out of the scene. Turn off the TV screen in your mind, breathe deeply again a couple of times, gently wiggle your arms and legs to get your circulation moving again, and slowly open your eyes.

Repeat this relaxation exercise whenever you need to each day. As you get used to it, you'll find it easier to do, and the images, sounds, and smells that you conjure up will become stronger and more vivid. You don't have to devote a lot of time—a couple of minutes spent in deep relaxation will bring hours of benefit. You can do the exercise in the train or bus on your way to work, while sitting at your desk or before you go into a meeting, when you get home at night, and at any other time when you need to relax.

GUIDELINES FOR RELAXATION

· Make time to be alone in a quiet place.
· Breathe deeply several times.
· Observe the muscles in your body as they relax.
· Imagine a beautiful scene in your mind's eye.
· Place yourself in the scene, relaxing.

VISUALIZATION

Many people with high-power or stressful jobs spend a few minutes relaxing at their desks several times a day. It increases their stamina and their ability to do their jobs well.

By the way, if you find it difficult to imagine a scene in your mind, look at a photograph of a favorite place and then close your eyes, and recreate that scene in your mind's eye.

How to Meditate

Meditation is a great way to improve and maintain your health and overall well-being. I recommend it to anyone.

Scientists are now beginning to study what happens to people when they meditate, and they have discovered that meditation can slow heart rate, regulate breathing, improve circulation, reduce stress, and make you feel good. They are proving scientifically what people who meditate have known for a long time!

The feeling you get from staring into your own eyes in a mirror (which I describe on pages 18–19), the comprehension that can come from it, is similar to the sensations that result when you meditate. Meditation is finding a quiet little corner of your mind, away from your surroundings, in which you can feel calm and completely relaxed. Many people are discouraged from meditating because they think it only works if they sit cross-legged on the floor, chant, or burn special candles. But you don't have to do any of those things. You can meditate just sitting in a chair if you wish, or even lying down. Choose a time when you won't be disturbed, and make yourself comfortable.

My technique is simple. First, I create a comfortable and quiet environment, with no phones ringing and no noise. Then I close

GUIDELINES FOR MEDITATION

- Make time to be alone in a quiet place.
- Breathe deeply several times.
- Observe the muscles in your body as they relax.
- Imagine positive energy around and in you.
- Reflect on your connection to the universe.
- Dispel all other thoughts.

my eyes, take a few moments to relax every part of my body, and let my mind drift. I let my inner energy leave me and travel into space. Inner energy is a powerful surge of knowledge—the awareness of a physical connection to an outside source of power. Some people may experience it as a warm sensation, others as a vibration or a tingling sensation. Some may hear sounds, such as a high-frequency hum or a high-pitched mantra. You may feel you are flying through space; imagine yourself doing this in your mind's eye, with the accompanying warmth, tingling, or high frequency. This out-of-the-body experience enables you to travel to any destination you desire in space. Don't fight it. Allow it to happen to you, allow your mind to let go and embark on an inner journey. If your mind becomes distracted by stray thoughts, take notice of them and then let them go.

When I meditate, it feels as if I am traveling through a host of tiny golden specks containing information and positive energy.

These particles of energy cling to me as I pass through them, and they are still with me when my mind returns from its journey. When you meditate, your brain may not be able to comprehend that this is happening, but that doesn't matter; you will be bringing back positive energy, which will refresh and cleanse you. It's almost as if you are leaving your body and washing yourself in a sea of golden particles of information, which gives you a pure sense of well-being, calmness, relaxation, awareness of God and the universe, and sense of your connection to your fellow living things on this planet. Whether you experience golden dots when you meditate or you see or feel things that are completely different doesn't matter—simply discover a way of meditation that works for you.

If you need help to clear or focus your mind, use the card with the orange meditation circle that comes with this kit. Hold it in front of you and look at it for a couple of minutes. Concentrate on the circle and nothing else. After a short time, your mind will detach itself. You can hold your crystal, the one that comes with the kit, and concentrate on the calming energy it gives you. This will enable you to tap into your awareness of another plane. You may find it hard to meditate easily at first, especially if your mind fills up with distracting thoughts, but after a while you will get used to it and start to notice the physical and mental benefits it gives you. Not only does meditation let you relax your body and mind completely, which reduces the negative effects of stress, but it also allows the right side of your brain—the creative, instinctive part—to be more open. You may find that you can solve problems more easily, that ideas come to you out of the blue, and that you have a more optimistic and enthusiastic outlook on life.

37

VISUALIZATION

When you have finished meditating you will be very relaxed. This is a good time to repeat your affirmations to yourself, if you wish. You will feel so relaxed that you may feel slightly dizzy if you stand up too quickly. Open your eyes slowly, stretch your limbs, and breathe normally for a couple of minutes before standing up.

WILLPOWER

~~~~~

How many times have you wanted to do something and not even tried, telling yourself, "I could do that if I only had the willpower"? Well, you have! We all have incredible willpower, but not everyone knows how to use it. That's why some people are able to achieve amazing feats while others can only marvel from the sidelines. Little do they know that they can do these things too!

Recently I was asked to activate the willpower of my local soccer team, Reading FC. The manager, John Madejski, is a friend of mine, and he was extremely anxious for the team to move up in the league standings. I attend all their home games when I'm in Britain, and I help the Reading team psych themselves up before each match by encouraging them to visualize themselves scoring goals and winning. They have just had their best season ever in the 124 years that they have been playing, and also their best standing ever in the Coca-Cola Cup, so I know that my techniques are having a tremendous effect. Waking up your willpower is like recharging a car battery. When the battery is dead, the car won't go anywhere, and you have to jumpstart it. The way to jumpstart your willpower is through devotion, discipline, determination, and passion. You must have discipline, you must be determined to reach your goals, and you must be passionately devoted to the way in which you achieve them. I can tell you now that if you don't have an inner conviction that you are going to meet your aims, you won't get anywhere. Willpower has nothing to do with being half-hearted. It's all about being single-minded—completely!

Laziness is the great enemy of willpower. Unfortunately, most of us are so deeply involved in our everyday lives that we don't make any effort to wake up our willpower, this energy that enables us to do all sorts of powerful, positive things. It's easier to tell ourselves that we'll give up smoking tomorrow, or that lots of other people are overweight, or that one chocolate cookie won't make any difference, or that, although we promised ourselves we'd exercise more, we'd better catch the bus instead of walking because it's raining. . . . We have all done it, even me. But no longer. Once I discovered what willpower could do for me, I never wanted to revert to my old, lazy ways.

In 1977, willpower saved my life. I was world-famous, had earned enough money to be very comfortable, and it seemed as if everything was going well for me. In fact, I was hiding a terrible secret. I had developed bulimia, the compulsive eating disorder that is an addiction of the highest degree, and it had been going on for a year. I would gorge myself on food, then disappear into the bathroom, stuff towels under the door so that no one could hear what was happening, and stick my fingers down my throat to make myself throw up. Then I would return to the table and carry on eating as if nothing at all had happened. At the time, Hanna was still living in Israel and I was in New York, but she used to visit me a lot, and she soon told me that I was looking terrible. I felt it, too.

Exercise has always been important to me. I like to keep fit, and it also helps boost my psychic powers. I was running every day, but I never kept my food down long enough to fuel my body. The result was that my weight was dropping fast—I lost thirty pounds. I was slowly starving myself to death, even though I was eating vast quantities of food. The end came one afternoon when I tried to get out of a car. To my horror, I had so little energy, I could barely heave myself out of my seat, and had to hold on to the roof of the car to yank myself up. The world spun, I felt dizzy and sick, my legs trembled, and at that moment I realized what I was doing to myself. I knew that if I didn't stop my bulimia immediately, it would kill me.

As soon as I was inside the house, I went into a quiet room by myself and shut the door. Then I summoned up all my psychic energy and repeated to myself over and over again, "I am going to stop my bulimia NOW. I am starting to regain my health NOW." It was like going cold turkey. I was trying to beat a life-threatening addiction, but I triggered my willpower to make my body get well again. That was the last day of being bulimic. I switched off the bulimic urges and blocked them whenever they threatened to come into my head. I repeated my mantra whenever I needed it, and it worked. I stopped the bulimia that very day. I just stopped, switched off, and never overate again. It wasn't easy, but I did it in one day. In this chapter, I am going to show you how to trigger your willpower and keep it active forever.

How to Activate Your Willpower

The first question to ask yourself is, "What do I want to achieve?" Do you want to lose weight? Do you want to succeed in life? Do you want to stop smoking? Stop taking drugs? Stop drinking? Stop biting your nails? Do you want to diminish your laziness, your apathy, your lack of responsibility for yourself? Once you have decided what it is that you want, you can start working toward achieving your goals. There is a particular way to achieve each goal, and I will be describing some of them in this chapter.

The next thing to do is to invent a resolution, a mantra, or an affirmation to help you achieve your aims. If you want to stop over-eating, your mantra might be "I eat when I am hungry" or "I do not eat fried foods." Choose a mantra that suits your needs, and be prepared to alter it whenever necessary to fit the situation. It's a great technique—all you do is repeat the mantra several times in your head and out loud when you can, two or three times a day. It ignites the dormant willpower in your brain and makes it work for you. The reason repeating your mantra over and over works is that the brain acts like a muscle: It requires training, or programming. Repetition trains the brain so that, eventually, what you are repeating becomes automatic.

When you create your mantra or affirmation, there are several techniques that you can use to ensure it's as powerful as possible. Many teachers of self-development believe that mantras should be positive and in the present tense. They should also include the word *me* or *I*, to make them as personal as possible. This way, they immediately trigger your subconscious into turning the message of your affirmation into reality. Instead of repeating a mantra that mentions the future, such as "In a month's time I will have lost fourteen pounds," choose one that is in the present tense, such as "I am reaching my target weight now." Remember too that the mantra should be as positive as possible. Try not to focus on the negative. For instance, instead of saying to yourself, "I am no longer fat," say something like "I am slim and healthy now."

You can repeat your affirmation while you are driving, walking, working, doing the wash, taking a shower, or whenever you walk past a pastry shop and feel an overpowering compulsion to go in and treat yourself to something. You don't have to spend very long saying your mantra, either. It might take one minute, or only several seconds. The important thing is to repeat the affirmation, because it is the key that will unlock your willpower. Once you have unlocked it, you can do anything.

You are going to need patience. If you have never done anything like this before, you may find it hard going at first, especially on bad days, when temptation seems almost irresistible. Learn to be patient, but at the same time tell yourself that you are going to succeed. Block out any nagging voices in your head that whisper otherwise. It may help to choose "All my affirmations succeed" as one of your mantras. It will also help if you distract yourself when you are really tempted to have a cigarette, eat a candy bar, or go on a spending spree. Do something else, block the temptation out of your mind, and think about other things. After a while, this will get easier and easier. Soon you will find that you go for whole hours, then whole days, without being tempted.

Before we go any further, I'd like to give you some advice. I feel rather sad at having to do it, but it is vitally important. Be careful whom you tell about your newfound desire to use willpower to stop smoking, lose weight, or do whatever else you want. If you tell someone who is negative, or envious because they'd like to do it but are too lazy, they will try to deter you, and their negativity will prevent you from achieving your goals. Achieve your goals and *then* tell everyone how you did it. They may still feel envious, but that is their problem, not yours.

WILLPOWER

Improve Your Self-Confidence

There are two ways to improve self-confidence—from the inside and from the outside. Let's take the outside first, because that is what other people see when they meet you. First impressions are important, so you have to make sure that your appearance acts as an advertisement for you. You want to promote the feel-good factor. Make sure that you look good, you smell nice, you are well-groomed, your hair is clean, your clothes are attractive and spotless, you are wearing the right colors for you, your shoes are in good repair, and you walk and talk nicely. If you achieve all these things, you will have a good basis for feeling confident.

Now let's think about boosting your confidence from the inside. All you have to do is talk yourself into being more confident. Say to yourself, "I have CONFIDENCE in myself, I have CONFIDENCE in myself," and suddenly you will be filled with a sense of power. You will feel strong, and that will project out to your family, friends, business partners, and the other people you encounter in your life. You might even wish to do this while standing in front of a mirror as described on page 19.

What you must never do is tell yourself that you would like to do something but that you would fail, and so you do not even bother to try doing it. How do you know that you would fail? The only failure lies in not trying. There are many people who work to achieve their dearest wish, whether it is breaking a world record or scoring a personal triumph, and they persist even if it will never make them famous or it takes their whole life.

An important point to remember is that having self-confidence doesn't mean being aggressive. It means having confidence in yourself and your abilities, and once you have that you can get on better with others because you are more relaxed and do not feel that you have to prove anything. It is only bullies who cover up their insecurity with rudeness and belligerence, who feel they have to show the world how clever and wonderful they think (or hope) they are.

Once you start to radiate confidence, you will begin to get positive feedback, and that will help boost your confidence even more. People may not praise you to your face, but you will be able to know how they feel about you from the way they treat you and, sometimes, the nice things they say about you to others. All those

TIPS ON BOOSTING YOUR SELF-CONFIDENCE

- Create an affirmation that makes you feel good about yourself—such as "I have CONFIDENCE in myself, I have CONFIDENCE in myself"—and repeat it whenever you need a boost.
- When your confidence flags, recall a situation in which you did really well. Remember how good you felt and recall the compliments you were paid.
- First impressions count for a lot, so make sure your appearance is as pleasant as possible.
- Before you attend important meetings or keep appointments, visualize yourself doing well.

good things will happen once you activate your mindpower into increasing your self-confidence.

So what do you do? Let's say you are about to go for a job interview. Look in the mirror beforehand and say to yourself, "I am well-qualified; I will do well at the interview." At the interview, greet everyone with a smile and a firm handshake. Afterward, praise yourself for doing your best at the interview. Why not? If you watch tennis you will see the top players egging themselves on, giving themselves pep talks on court, and then congratulating themselves

---

Rehearse your performance in your mind, concentrating on such positive points as people greeting you warmly and the discussion going well. If you've got to make a speech or present your ideas, picture yourself doing so and then imagine being praised.

- Congratulate yourself whenever you do something well.
- Learn to accept compliments instead of shrugging them off or making light of your achievements.
- Be yourself, and let your natural charm shine through.
- Remember that positive thoughts attract positive results.

~~~~

whenever they win a difficult point or a match. They pat their tennis rackets or applaud themselves, and you can do the same. Congratulate yourself when you do something well! After all, you probably tell yourself off when you do something badly, so why not take time to praise yourself too? It won't give you a big head, but it will give you an increased sense of self-worth and self-confidence and have a powerful and positive effect on you.

Don't forget the other important rule in boosting your self-confidence—use your charm. Be likable, positive, and courteous, and don't lose your sense of humor by taking everything, including yourself, too seriously. Some people have natural charisma; others have to work at it. Don't get charisma confused with good looks, because they don't always go hand in hand. We have all met people who wouldn't win any beauty contests but have such attractive personalities that we don't notice their physical flaws. Equally, we have all met people who are so good-looking they stop traffic but who are a washout when it comes to radiating charm and personality.

Beat Negative Thinking

You would be astonished if you knew how damaging negative thinking can be. If you clutter your thoughts with negative images and ideas, such as always getting down on yourself by dwelling on your faults and failings or refusing to acknowledge your positive points, you will soon start to believe yourself. On the other hand, if you believe in yourself, congratulate yourself whenever you do well, and invoke your willpower to achieve the things you want to do, you will radiate positive energy both inwardly and outwardly.

Negative thinking can destroy relationships, marriages, jobs, health, and peace of mind. We all know people who are nitpickers, who always find fault with things and for whom nothing is ever good enough. When you are about to meet someone like this, do you eagerly look forward to that meeting, or does your heart sink at the prospect of having to listen to another long list of complaints? (And do you ever wonder what they might be saying about you behind your back?) Be honest with yourself. If you do enjoy being with someone negative, ask yourself why. Is it because they are doing all the moaning for you, or is it because they appeal to your negative side? These people are usually miserable and unhappy, and, unfortunately, they often transfer that misery to you because you absorb it like a sponge. You may find that once you start to control your own negative thinking, you will no longer want these people to play such an important role in your life. As you become more positive, you will start to attract more positive people to you. The moaners and groaners of this world will soon get fed up with your cheerful smile and ability to look on the bright side and will have to start looking for someone new to depress.

How do you view your life? How do you view your future? If you tend to be pessimistic, you are already building up a negative image of your future, but how do you know what's going to happen? None of us know what's around the corner, because life is so full of surprises. However, one thing's for sure—if you spend your life feeling negative and thinking that bad things are going to happen to you, they probably will. There are two reasons for that. First, you may be so locked into being negative that you ignore the good things in your life and focus on the bad—you are always looking for the cloud around the silver lining. Second, we attract what we give out, so if you send out negative vibrations all the time, they are what you will receive. At a very simple level, if you are grumpy or bad-tempered with people they will usually respond to you in the same way. But if you are good-natured and greet people with a genuine smile, they will normally respond in an equally friendly way. If you don't believe me, try it and see. You will be amazed.

The fallout from negative thinking is incredibly damaging, both mentally and physically. It literally puts a lot of pressure on you mentally, because all those dark thoughts will interfere with your energy patterns and press down on you. That's why we say we

TIPS ON BEATING NEGATIVE THINKING

·   Whenever you catch yourself putting yourself down, stop that thought and replace it with an affirmation that boosts your confidence and self-esteem.

·   Stop focusing on the things that have gone wrong in your life and concentrate instead on the things that have been a success.

·   Learn to let go of the past. If you often replay unhappy or disastrous events in your mind, accept that they're in the past and you can't do anything to change them. Learn any lessons that these experiences are teaching you, then picture yourself

are depressed—our spirits are being squashed by our negative emotions. Physically, depression makes you feel tired and listless. Your
limbs ache, everything is too much effort, you lose sleep, you can't
be bothered to eat properly or you eat the wrong things, you wake
up in the middle of the night worrying. If things get really bad you
might start suffering from panic attacks, which can completely dis-
rupt your life. Negativity also puts you under stress or adds to your
existing stress, and we all know by now that stress can cause a
whole range of symptoms, illnesses, and diseases, from headaches

putting them in a box, slamming the lid, and
vaporizing them.

- If you're worried or anxious about something, allow
yourself only five minutes a day of worrying time.
After that, block off those worries and make yourself think about something else.

- Understand and accept that negative thoughts
attract negative results. Think about possible ways
in which this is working in your life, and resolve to
change negative thoughts into positive ones.

- Confiding your troubles in a sympathetic listener
will put them into perspective. Be prepared to
return the favor if necessary.

and colds to potentially life-threatening conditions such as cancer, stomach ulcers, and heart disease.

How do you deal with your own negative thinking? Imagine that your mind is a nuclear power station, and your negative thoughts are the nuclear reactor that has to be isolated whenever it overheats to stop its causing dangerous contamination. In your case, overheating means thinking negatively or feeling depressed. You have to learn to isolate your negative thoughts whenever they threaten to contaminate your life.

My technique is to choose a set time every day when I can talk to myself about my negative thoughts and deal with them so they won't spill over into my other daily activities. When I have finished my conversation with myself, I put my negative thoughts in a separate room in my mind. The trick is to know how to shut the door on that room and not let those negative thoughts escape. It is important for you to have control over them, rather than the other way around. Choose a time in the day when your friends and family are busy or occupied, take the phone off the hook or switch on the answering machine, and go into a quiet room by yourself. If you have a hectic life, you might find that the only time you have to yourself is when you are in the bath or shower, but that's okay. Let your negative thoughts flow out, and listen carefully to them. Start to analyze them. "Why am I thinking about that? Do I need to think about that? Is it important enough? If so, why? Am I overestimating its importance?" Once you start to do this, you will be amazed at how many of your negative thoughts will diminish and then disappear. You will be able to sift through them and sort out the real problems from the minor niggles of everyday life that you have blown out of all proportion, like turning ants into elephants. The difference it will make to your life will be astounding.

However, don't try to do this exercise when you wake up in the middle of the night, because that's the time when the smallest worry can become magnified. If that happens to you a lot, or you go through a period when you lie awake every night fretting about your life, you must imagine putting those worries into a box and slamming the lid on them. Tell yourself firmly that you will deal with those concerns in the morning, but that now you are going to go back to sleep. If your mind strays back to the worries, repeat to yourself that you will deal with them in the morning, and you are now going to sleep. You can even use mantras to make yourself go to sleep if you wish. Try something like "I am going to sleep NOW, I am going to sleep NOW." When I can't sleep, I visualize a big light switch over the bed, and mentally I flick it off, telling myself that with it I am switching off my mind and I will now go to sleep. At that point, I fall into a deep, refreshing sleep. Try it for yourself—it does work!

Once you start practicing this technique of locking your problems away in a box, you will find that many of them solve themselves. Some will simply vanish, and the solutions to others will suddenly drop, fully formed, into your mind; your subconscious will have been working away on them without your conscious mind realizing it. Your brain is capable of much more than you know.

Another good way of dealing with negative thinking is to confide in someone whose opinion you trust and who you know will listen. (Trying to talk to someone who is more interested in having his or her say than in listening to you will make you feel even more upset than you were to begin with.) Share your negative thoughts about yourself, your worries about your future, your fears about your family, or whatever else is bothering you. Getting problems off your chest will enable you to put them into perspective and deal with them. If the problem is extremely personal and you are hiding it from the world, you will have to deal with it on your own unless it is something with such potential to harm you that you really should confide in someone.

If you have had a terrible day and feel that you will explode unless you can tell your partner or friend all about what's bugging you, but you don't want to go on and on about it all evening, set a time limit for your tale of woe. Set a stopwatch or alarm clock to ring in five or ten minutes, and concentrate on getting it all off your chest. Say how you really feel, what a bad day you've had and why, and stop when time's up. You'll feel much better, and then you can get on with talking about or doing something more enjoyable. Get rid of your irritation and move on!

Physical therapy can also help enormously in dispelling worries and working off pent-up anger. Lose yourself in something you really enjoy, such as gardening, carpentry, walking the dog, making some bread, jogging, or taking up a new hobby—the list is endless. It can be especially satisfying if all your hard work produces something that is of help to others.

Stop Smoking

Many smokers have no idea of the damage that cigarettes do to their bodies. Are you the same? You might read alarming articles in the newspapers, but after feeling worried for a while you tell yourself to dismiss the stories, or try to think of someone you know who

WILLPOWER

has smoked all his or her life and doesn't show any ill effects. It's easy to give yourself excuses for not stopping. I have never smoked, but I have helped lots of smokers to beat this awful habit. In my experience the best way to do that is to show them the evidence of what cigarettes do to our bodies.

When I give a lecture onstage, I usually ask, "Who wants to stop smoking tonight?" I always see hundreds of people raising their hands. I take out a cigarette and light it, take a puff, and blow the smoke into a white handkerchief. Then I show the audience the handkerchief, stained with black, tarry residue, and say, "Look at what you are doing to yourselves." Then I tell the audience what I want them to do. I count up to three, and they must shout, "I stop smoking TONIGHT!" I am able to trigger the willpower of about one-quarter of the smokers in the audience by this one simple sentence, and they stop smoking on that day. This is because they are now able to talk to themselves, and they will always hear that phrase.

Another important step in quitting smoking is to think about the effects your cigarette smoke has on the people around you. It has been proven that cigarette smoke harms others who have to breathe it, so do you really want to hurt the people you love by puffing harmful cigarette smoke all over them? Once you start to realize that you are damaging other people with your cigarette smoke, you will find it easier to beat the craving.

I believe that only losers smoke. A lot of people get offended when I tell them that they are losers, and they usually start to assure me of how successful they are. Then, when they go home, they start thinking and realize that I was right—they are losers because they are doing something bad to their bodies. They may be intelligent, but they are behaving stupidly. To give up smoking, you can

---

TIPS FOR STOPPING SMOKING

- Blow your cigarette smoke into a clean white handkerchief, look at it, and realize that your lungs are coated with the tar and nicotine that you see there, only in a much greater volume.
- Throw away any cigarettes you have lying around the house.
- Repeat your mantra several times every day.
- Tell yourself that you want to be a winner, not a loser.
- Sniff an ashtray full of cigarette butts. Ask yourself if you want your breath, hair, and clothes to smell like that any longer.

---

repeat to yourself, "I don't want to be a loser, I want to be a winner." Winners are usually intelligent people who know about life, are well educated, well read. How can a winner smoke? I doubt that any of the ten most successful men in America smoke. Sure, there are people who are successful and who smoke, but they may not have many years left in which to enjoy their wealth and success because they may die early from cancer, a stroke, heart disease, or another smoking-related illness.

Many people are put off by the idea of giving up smoking because they are worried that they will gain weight. If you belong in

- Realize that you are harming your loved ones' health, particularly your children's, by smoking around them.
- Visualize yourself no longer wanting to smoke. Imagine refusing a cigarette when one is offered to you. Practice this every day, especially before you go to a party or a bar where you know you will be tempted.
- Visualize how healthy and energetic you will feel when your body has rid itself of the toxins and nicotine introduced by smoking.
- Imagine your lungs and your heart looking fresh, pink, and healthy.

this category, the next section in this chapter should be interesting reading!

Control Your Weight

There's only one thing that makes us put on weight, and that's food. If you overeat and consume more calories than your body can burn up, you put on weight. If the number of calories that you consume equals the number of calories you burn up, you will stay at your present weight. If you take in fewer calories than you burn

TIPS FOR LOSING WEIGHT

- Repeat your affirmation several times each day.
- Congratulate yourself when you make progress.
- Increase the amount of exercise you do each day. Brisk walking is one of the best ways to burn calories. Keep picturing in your mind the way you will look when you've reached your target weight.
- Enjoy the knowledge that you are in control of your body at last. Tell yourself you will never let your body control you again.
- When you are tempted to binge on food or eat something that will break your diet, say to

up every day, you will lose weight. It's as simple as that.

Where food is concerned, the world is divided into two kinds of people. There are those who eat to live and those who live to eat. The people who belong in the first category are rarely overweight; they are able to tune into the messages their bodies are giving them, so they eat when they are hungry and stop when they are full. They may really enjoy their food, but it doesn't rule their lives. They are in control of it. It's the people who live to eat who have lost their control over food. They are often overweight, yet they continue to eat too much, telling themselves, "You only live once." Unfortunately, that may turn out to be only a brief life, because yourself, "I will NOT eat this. I do NOT need to eat this."

- If you have a terrible craving for a piece of chocolate cake or a big lump of cheese, imagine that you are eating it. Picture it in front of you, smell it, then imagine putting it in your mouth. Concentrate on the flavors, the textures. Really revel in them. Chew, then swallow your imaginary food. Tell yourself that you have satisfied that craving, then go and do something unconnected with food. It works!
- Think slim!

overweight people are at greater risk of developing high blood pressure, diabetes, and gall bladder disease, and they can fatally strain their hearts by having to carry around so much extra weight. Problems with joints, such as arthritis, are also made worse because of overweight. There are many other drawbacks. Your clothes don't fit properly; you get out of breath easily; you don't look very attractive when naked; you feel out of condition; you have to drag yourself around; and you may share others' low opinion of yourself for getting so big. Yet you probably say, "I just don't have the willpower to lose weight" as you reach for another slice of cake, or put a blob of butter on your potatoes. Well, I can assure you that you do have the willpower! Everyone has the willpower. All you need to do is find the key to developing it, which is how this kit can help you.

All the information contained in this section is based on plain common sense, but please consult your doctor before starting a weight-loss program or changing your diet if you are worried about your health in any way, have gained a lot of weight in a very short

ADDITIONAL TIPS FOR WEIGHT CONTROL

- Never go food shopping when you are hungry—you will buy more food than you need, and you might also buy a high-calorie snack to eat on the way home.
- Take only the amount of money you know you will need to pay for the groceries. If you take more money, you are likely to splurge on "forbidden" foods.
- Never eat standing up, or when reading or watching TV. Always sit at your kitchen or dining room table and concentrate on your food so you can get the most satisfaction from it.
- Chew each mouthful slowly.

time, are suffering from a long-term illness, have recently had major surgery, or have a heart condition. You should also see your doctor if you are planning to do a lot of exercise when your body is not used to it.

If you want to control your weight, the first thing you need is a good mirror, full-length if possible. Take off your clothes and stand

- Always get up from the table feeling as if you've still got some room left in your stomach.
- Buy yourself a good book listing the calories in every food you eat.
- Do not allow yourself snacks between meals, and do not finish off leftovers while clearing the table. You can consume up to 1,000 extra calories per day by nibbling between meals and eating snacks.
- Read the labels and nutritional information on packaged foods, and avoid those with excess or hidden sugar, salt, or fat.
- When making a sandwich, butter only one piece of bread, or omit butter entirely in sand-wiches with fatty fillings such as peanut butter or soft cheese.

in front of the mirror in a good light. Do this first thing in the morning, rather than at night, when your stomach will probably still be full from dinner. Take a long, hard look at yourself, starting with your face and working all the way down to your toes. What do you like about your body? Maybe you have lovely eyes, good broad shoulders, or a trim waist. Take time to appreciate these parts of yourself. Look at yourself again, this time studying the parts you don't like. (By the way, don't forget to look at yourself sideways!) Maybe you're starting to develop a double chin, there is much more of your tummy than there used to be, or what was once an hourglass figure has turned into something that looks more like Humpty-Dumpty. Before you start to feel too depressed about the current you, imagine how you will look when you have lost a little weight and rediscovered your hips, or eliminated that unflattering bulge around your tummy. Imagine how good you will feel about yourself, how good your clothes will look, how wonderful it will be when your waistband is no longer tight, how you will enjoy being able to wear the clothes that are hanging in the back of your closet because you can't squeeze into them any longer. Keep these thoughts in your head, because they are incentives that will help you to tap into your willpower.

Now set goals, target weight-loss points. It is important that your goals be realistic; otherwise, you may easily be discouraged. You must take it one step at a time. For instance, if you are thirty pounds overweight, make your first target losing ten pounds gradually, preferably at no more than two pounds per week. (An unsupervised weight loss of more than this per week can do you more harm than good.) When you have achieved your first goal and lost ten pounds, you can congratulate yourself heartily and set yourself your next target, which is to lose another ten pounds. When that is gone, you can give yourself a real pat on the back and set about shedding those final ten pounds. That sounds much more manageable, doesn't it, than telling yourself at the outset that you are going to lose thirty pounds? If you set yourself such an enormous target, you stand less chance of achieving it because it may quickly seem almost unattainable.

There is another important point that I want you to consider. You may dream of having a body like Cher's or Sylvester Stallone's, but you will never be able to look like them if you are five feet tall with big bones, a wide pelvis, and narrow shoulders. All the willpower in the world won't change your basic body shape, unfortunately. But that doesn't mean you can't make the best of what you've been given and look as good as possible.

So how are you going to use willpower to control your weight? What you have got to do is talk to yourself, three or four times a day, choosing a mantra or resolution that fits your needs. Say, "I do NOT eat any more chocolate." Say, "I do NOT eat food that I know makes me fat." Say, "I STICK to my diet. I STICK to my diet. It is going to WORK for me." Not many people do this, simply because they don't know how effective this inner talk can be for them. In case you are thinking, "It's okay for Uri, because he's slim," let me tell you that I used to be an overweight couch potato, and that it was willpower that helped me overcome my bulimia, get healthy, and stay fit. It worked for me and it will work for you.

Repeat your mantra each day, and obey it, respect it, believe it. Visualize the slim you. After a couple of weeks, seeing *will* be believing because you will be able to look in the mirror and see the results. Then you can reward yourself with little treats, such as a new sweater or shirt, that will give you the incentive to carry on. Think slim! Strengthen your inner power, awaken your willpower and discipline.

When you reach your target, the first thing to do is to congratulate yourself, and the second thing is to work out how you are going to keep your weight at this level and not let it start creeping up again. And that's where self-love comes in. If you love yourself, you will love the new you. Tell yourself, "Today is the beginning of the new me. This is how I love looking. This is how I will stay for the rest of my life." Repeat this affirmation to yourself several times a day, and let your willpower continue to work for you. It will help you keep your ideal weight and stop you from gaining weight again.

Strange as it may seem, you may find that not everyone is as delighted as you are with your new, slim shape. You may have to deal with jealousy from lots of people, whether it comes from colleagues, so-called friends, or even your partner. Don't listen! If you love yourself, you will protect yourself against people who want to put you down.

Stick to Any Exercise Program

We hear more and more about the dangers of not getting enough exercise, from stories about children who are becoming unfit and overweight because of their sedentary lifestyles to adults who rarely do anything more strenuous than climb in and out of their cars. If you are aware that you need more exercise, remember its many benefits. Not only can it help you become fitter, it can also help you lose weight, feel healthier, and enjoy better sleep. What's more, your mental state will improve, and you will feel more relaxed. In other words, exercise can help you combat stress.

For many people, however, knowing that exercise is good for them is one thing, but doing something about it is quite another. It's easy to make excuses, such as lack of time or lack of opportunity, for not getting more exercise. But exercise exists in many forms. Even simple things such as walking to local stores or the post office instead of driving or taking the stairs instead of the elevator can have a beneficial impact on your health. Other things you can do include becoming involved in a sport you enjoy, which will make you want to stick with it, or buying or renting exercise videos and following them at home.

No matter what kind of exercise you wish to pursue, you will need to create positive affirmations to help you stick to your program. Choose an affirmation that is perfectly suited to your needs. For example, "I STICK to my exercise program. It is WORKING for me." You can also try, "I am ENJOYING my exercise program. I LOVE the results I'm getting. I feel FANTASTIC from exercise." Repeat these mantras whenever you need a boost to your flagging willpower. If you catch yourself thinking something like, "I don't think I'll do my exercises today, I just can't be bothered," instantly follow that thought with your affirmation and be sure to really believe in what you are saying. Also, spend time visualizing yourself enjoying your exercises and the benefits from exercise. This will put you in the right frame of mind to want to continue with your program.

Healthful Eating

Of course, it is not only willpower that you need to lose weight— you also need to stick to a healthful diet. After all, there is no point

HOW TO BE MORE HEALTHY

- Stand straight. Lots of people slouch or have rounded shoulders, without realizing it. So stand in front of your mirror and scrutinize yourself. Are you slouching or slumped? Now stand straighter. Can you see the difference? Your tummy and bottom become smaller, you look as if you have already lost weight, you instantly feel more positive and dynamic, and your lungs and digestive system will work more effectively.
- Walk whenever possible. Leave your car at home and walk to the store, to buy the paper, or to visit your friends. If you travel by bus, get off one stop before your usual one.

in repeating your dieting affirmation to yourself several times a day if you are still gorging yourself on french fries or brownies. You have to help yourself—and I'm not talking about the cookie jar!

The problem for many people is that they've tried diets in the past, but in the end they always regained the weight they had lost. That's hardly surprising. The latest research is proving that some diets can actually make you fat. Any crash diet that suddenly robs you of all the calories, fats, and nutrition that you used to eat and replaces them with half a grapefruit or a glass of carrot juice and nothing else will eventually send emergency signals shooting to

- Take the stairs instead of the elevator, and walk up or down escalators instead of standing still.
- Eat at least five pieces of fresh fruit and vegetables, preferably organic, each day.
- Eat plenty of fiber in order to help your body rid itself of toxins and waste matter.
- Drink plenty of fluids each day to flush out your kidneys, plump up your skin, and keep the whites of your eyes clear.
- Enjoy your newfound feeling of improved health. Congratulate yourself on the progress you've made so far.
- Think positively—which is what this kit is all about.

your brain, telling your body that it is being starved. The result is that your body will conserve all the calories it receives and store them as fat because it won't know when it will next get a decent meal, rather like someone stocking up their larder before a siege. So you will start to put on weight again, and that is the last thing you want. The secret to losing weight is by harnessing your willpower to do it gradually. Eat sensibly and adopt a proper eating plan for life. Forget about those diets that have you living on nothing but oranges or watercress or rare steak, and start learning to reeducate your body about the food it needs.

If you have ever accidentally put diesel fuel into a car that takes gas, then tried to start the car, you will know the result—nothing happens. Our bodies are much more complicated than a car engine, but they work on the same principle—they need decent fuel in order to operate efficiently. That is why athletes prepare themselves for a big race or important match by eating the right foods. They choose foods that are high in complex carbohydrates, such as pasta, because the body burns this fuel slowly and steadily as it needs energy. What they don't do is eat three bars of chocolate followed by a couple of doughnuts. If you have ever had a meal like that you'll know why. You might feel great at first, but after a while you will start to feel exhausted, unsatisfied, and slightly sick. That is because you have overloaded your bloodstream with sugar, which triggers your body to process that sugar as soon as possible before it does you any harm. Your blood sugar level drops sharply and you need more food to get it back to normal, so you grab a pastry or some cookies to tide you over until your next meal. The more sugar you eat, the more sugar you crave, and the more your weight goes up. Believe me, sugar can be as addictive as nicotine or alcohol.

If you are unsure about which foods are good for you and which are junk, then I suggest you read some good books on the subject. The secret of healthful eating is moderation. Whether you are a meat eater, a vegetarian, or a vegan, you will never be fat or unhealthy if you eat a good variety of foods in moderation.

To me, a healthy diet involves cutting back on cholesterol, which you find particularly in egg yolks, animal fats, and dairy produce; cutting out all red meat; eating lots and lots of fresh (preferably organic) fruit and vegetables; eating plenty of complex carbohydrates such as bread, rice, pasta, and potatoes; eating plenty of fiber; cutting back on sugar and salt; and drinking fruit juices and water rather than alcohol and fizzy, sugary drinks.

Breakfast is a very important meal. If you are using your willpower to lose weight, you will be making life unnecessarily hard for yourself if you cut out breakfast. It is said that you should breakfast like an emperor, lunch like a king, and dine like a pauper—in other words, you should make breakfast your biggest meal of the day. However, that is just not possible for many people because of the way their lives are structured. Even if you have only a couple of slices of toast or a bowl of cereal in the morning, however, you will stay even-tempered and boost your brainpower. What's more, it is less likely that you will be tempted into having a midmorning snack if you are still full from breakfast. Can't face food first thing? Then have your breakfast or a sandwich later on in the morning when your digestion has settled down—it will do you much more good than reaching for some cookies or a bag of chips.

The food industry is worth billions of dollars each year, so it is hardly surprising that we are always being bombarded with new information and scare stories about particular foods. One of the most recent surveys has claimed that drinking alcohol every day can prevent heart disease, but it says nothing about the damage it can do to your liver. It is just one example of the way you need to exercise your common sense and remember that moderation in all things is the key to keeping healthy.

Some people believe that you have to eat meat every day to stay fit, look good, and keep your muscles toned. I don't agree at all! I have been a vegetarian for over seventeen years, yet my muscles are strong—which is just as well, since I ride about fifty miles on my exercise bike every morning—and I am extremely fit. Of course, it is up to you to decide whether or not you want to give up meat. You can always have some meatless days each week if you want to see what a vegetarian diet is like.

Diet affects your brain as well as your body. The latest research has shown that what appear to be the early symptoms of Alzheimer's disease—confusion and loss of memory—are reversed when the patient eats a balanced diet. I think this makes perfect sense, because I don't believe you can isolate one part of your body from another when something goes wrong. If you aren't eating properly, it is hardly surprising that your brain will not work as it should.

I am a great believer in vitamins, and I take many different supplements each day. I don't want to turn everyone into health freaks, but I think it is important to take a multivitamin and vitamin C every day. And if you are a vegetarian, I would also recommend vitamin B12.

I have spent a lot of time talking about the importance of a healthful diet, but I can assure you that improving your well-being is not a massive undertaking. There are many simple things you can do to get fit and boost your willpower. Once you begin to feel the effects of your new way of life, you will never want to revert to the old, sluggish you.

Control the Aging Process

First of all, I am sorry to say that there are no magic potions to stop your body from getting older. Besides, if there were any such potions, can you imagine how much they would cost? Everyone would want to buy them, and the manufacturers would be sitting on a gold mine.

WILLPOWER

Some beauty companies are now producing lotions and creams that they claim will slow down the aging process, although some of these claims have yet to be validated conclusively by scientists. I prefer two other ways of keeping myself looking young. One of them is conventional and one is unconventional, and I use them in conjunction with each other.

The conventional way is to ensure that I eat a healthful, balanced diet, get plenty of exercise and a good night's sleep, use a good skin moisturizer, and keep out of the sun, which can cause premature wrinkles.

The unconventional method is mirroring. I talk to my body in the mirror. I stare into my eyes and say, "I am now going to talk to myself." I then instruct each part of my body to slow down its aging process. You can do this in your head or out loud. Talk to your body, your skin, your blood cells, your muscles, your eyes, your hair, your liver, your kidneys, your heart, and your lungs, and tell them all to slow down. Say, "Don't age on me, slow down." You will be virtually hypnotizing your own DNA system, your chromosomes and the billions of cells in your body. Scientists have discovered that the body renews all its cells every seven years, so who is to say that you can't take that one step farther by talking to those cells and instructing them to slow down the aging process? After all, the human body is a miracle machine, and we should never underestimate its hidden power. You will understand this better if you imagine your body as a network controlled by your brain. Think of all the processes that go on inside you without your being aware of them. The way your heart beats and pushes the blood around your body, the way your lungs operate, the way your digestive system processes your food, extracting all the nutrients before discarding anything it does not need. Unless something goes wrong, you are never consciously aware of everything going on inside you, yet, unconsciously, you have no doubt that your body is operating smoothly. So why shouldn't the messages you give your brain be transmitted to the relevant part of your body?

I am quite convinced that mirroring works for me, so there is no reason why it should not do so for you. What have you got to lose? I look at my male friends and see that about 90 percent of them are losing their hair. Most of my friends who are younger than me are going gray. A few years ago, I realized that I was also starting to go gray. However, I was determined to reverse the process, and I managed to do it by talking to myself and also increasing my intake of the vitamins and vitamin components—biotin, inositol, folic acid, pantothenic acid, and PABA—which affect the amount of pigmentation in hair. Despite the fact that I have always had excellent eyesight, in 1985 I found that my vision was no longer perfect. I decided to take more beta carotene and vitamin E in addition to talking to my eye muscles, and my eyesight immediately went back to normal. However, I did first see an optometrist to check that my failing eyesight was being caused by age and not an illness, and it is important that you do the same before you try to heal yourself of any complaint. Once your doctor has checked that there is nothing seriously wrong, you can start to talk your body into becoming young once more. And you won't need any cosmetic surgery in order to do it!

COLOR THERAPY

~~~~

W e take many things for granted in our lives, including the wonderful effects of color. As you become more psychic and your mind power expands, not only will you become more sensitive to color, you will want to harness the power of color in your life. If you have never considered the beneficial effects of color before, I would like you to read this chapter with an open mind and think carefully about what I say.

Some Other Rainbow, by John McCarthy and Jill Morrell, describes McCarthy's experiences during the five years that he was a hostage. Reading the book is an incredible, thought-provoking experience, but I was particularly struck by McCarthy's description of the day he and his co-captive, Brian Keenan, were given a bowl of cherries by their captors. Although they had existed on a dreary diet for years, they waited for days before eating the cherries because they could not stop looking at their fantastic color. They feasted their eyes on them for a long time before feasting their stomachs. I have also heard that when prisoners of war are released from captivity, one of the ways they are helped to come to terms with their experiences and reintegrate themselves into the world is through color; they are given books containing nothing but pages full of color. Color can have powerful healing effects.

I'm not going to go into long, complicated explanations about how we are able to see color; I'm not a scientist, and some excellent books have already been written on the subject if you want to know more. What I want to talk about in this chapter is how I have used color and I believe you can use color in positive ways to enrich the quality of your life, improve your health, boost your self-confidence, empower yourself, and increase your energy. If you don't believe that such things are possible, read on!

The Orange Circle

If you haven't yet read my chapter on psychokinesis (see pages 125–31), you won't know how to use the orange circle that comes with this kit. Take it out now and study it. Look at its wonderfully bright color and see how it affects your mood. You will probably feel energized just by looking at it. Do you feel warmer, more positive, happier? In a moment I will tell you what this orange circle can do for you, but first I want to tell you why I think orange is such an important color. Orange, as you probably know, is a blend of the colors yellow and red. What you may not know is that yellow is the color of mental energy and red of physical energy. Orange fills you with inspiration and gives you the energy to act on it. Next time you are stumped for an idea or draw a mental blank, you could concentrate on this orange dot, relax your body, and wait for the ideas to flow. I can assure you they will!

Like the crystal that comes with this kit, the orange circle is fully charged with my psychic powers, ready for you to use them. All you need to do to activate them is sit quietly in a room where you won't be disturbed, then place your hands on the orange meditation circle and stroke it gently for about three minutes. While you are doing this, think of all the fantastic things you want to attract into your life. Money, health, happiness, success in school for

WAYS TO USE COLOR IN YOUR LIFE

- Wear the color that has the right healing properties for you.
- Decorate your home in the right colors for you.
- Visualize a particular color whenever you need it.
- Eat foods that are the color you need.
- Fill vases with flowers in suitable colors.
- Choose paintings and posters full of the colors you need.
- Meditate on the color of your choice.
- Use my orange dot to attract good fortune and health into your life.
- Combat pain by visualizing the affected area being saturated with a suitable color.

your children, a better job—whatever it is you want, think hard about it. By the way, the orange dot won't work if you try to imagine negative things, such as triumphing over a colleague, snubbing someone, or hoping that bad things will happen. It only works when you wish for *positive* things.

The second way the orange circle works is described in detail on page 75–76. When combined with the psychic powers that you are working to develop, the orange circle can help you to achieve things that you would once have thought impossible, such as mending broken watches and clocks.

Bringing Color into Your Life

As you probably know, the color spectrum consists of seven main colors—red, orange, yellow, green, blue, indigo, and violet. But did you know that each of these colors has a particular energy and therefore exerts a different influence over our bodies? Maybe you've noticed this yourself—have you found that if you wear a certain color or colors you feel energized, optimistic, happy, and able to cope with whatever pitfalls life places in your path, whereas there are other colors you avoid because they always make you feel depressed, pessimistic, lacking in energy and off-color?

Did you notice that word I just used? Off-color, meaning not very well? Think of all the other phrases involving color we use to describe our emotions. We say we're in the pink when we're feeling great, in a brown study when we're lost in thought, in a black mood when we're depressed, or feeling blue when we're melancholic, and when we do something that annoys someone we say it's like a red rag to a bull. Well, all these phrases reflect our subconscious knowledge of what different colors mean. In this chapter I want to make you conscious of that knowledge so you can put it into practice for yourself. Color helps to activate the mind's untapped potential.

The Color Spectrum

Here's a brief description of the main characteristics of each color so you can see the areas of life, the emotions, and the parts of your body that it influences. Think about each color and decide whether it works for you in the ways that I describe here—everyone has different needs and ideas, so you may find that some of what I write about red, perhaps, is more the way you feel about green, or blue affects you in the way I describe yellow will. Well, that's okay—simply follow your own instincts and use the color in the way that feels right for you.

RED. This is the most energetic color of all! You know the saying that redheads have fiery tempers? Well, maybe that's because red is the color associated with Mars, the god of war, and the planet Mars, the red planet. Red is the color of power. Red is a great color to wear when you are feeling lethargic, lacking in energy, or sluggish because it boosts your energy level and releases adrenaline into your bloodstream. However, it's not necessarily a good color to wear when you're feeling shy, because red will make you stand out from the crowd and throw you into the spotlight, and that may make you feel even more shy than before.

If you suffer from poor circulation or have cold hands and feet in the winter, try wearing red socks and gloves—they'll soon make you feel much warmer. Red is also a great color to choose for workout clothes such as sweat pants and leotards because it has such a powerfully energizing effect on the muscles. You can also close your eyes and visualize the color you want to boost your energy level.

ORANGE. This is a very significant color for me, as I have explained. And if you have already experimented with the orange meditation circle that comes with this kit, it may be a significant color for you. Orange has many of the qualities of red, such as stimulating the body's circulatory system, releasing adrenaline, and filling you with energy and enthusiasm. If you've got a lackluster attitude toward life, or you feel you're missing out on the enjoyments of life in some way, you need to introduce more orange into your world. As mentioned earlier, because there is yellow in it, orange also stimulates your mind, so it's a great color to keep near you when you are working. Wear an orange scarf or orange underwear and keep the orange circle close by you whenever you need to have your mind and body stimulated by the wonderful rays of the color orange.

YELLOW. This is a fantastic color if you want to stimulate your mental powers, because it represents the mind and the intellect. Ancient Chinese philosophers would refer to the golden mean when speaking of the importance of having a balanced mind. Keep a few yellow ornaments on your desk, or pin a predominantly yellow poster on a nearby wall so you can gaze at it whenever you are trying to come up with new ideas or need to give your brainpower a boost. But don't use too much yellow; it can make you feel quite detached from your surroundings, and that may make you lose touch with reality. However, if forgetting about reality for a while is just what you want because everything is getting on top of you and you're feeling stressed, wrap yourself in a yellow blanket or relax in a room filled with yellow, and you'll be able to forget about your cares for a while. You will benefit from it especially if you suffer from skin complaints such as acne or eczema or your joints are stiff.

Don't worry if yellow doesn't suit you when you wear it. Instead, cover your favorite chair with a fabric that has lots of yellow in it, buy yellow towels, flannels, and soap for the bathroom, and spend time in the sunshine (but do make sure you protect your skin from harmful ultraviolet rays). Finally, remember that you can always fill your mind with thoughts of yellow whenever you need positive mental energy.

GREEN. This is the fourth of the seven colors of the spectrum, which means it is the middle color. It is neither hot like red, orange, and yellow nor cold like blue, violet, and indigo. Green is the perfect color for integrating different energies and creating balance in your life. Maybe that is why many things in nature are green—because they represent what is in perfect balance.

Green is an extremely soothing color, which is why you will feel happier or more relaxed if you go for a walk in the countryside or sit for a while in a beautiful garden. Even stretching out full-length on the grass will help to balance your emotions, bring you down to earth (in this case literally!), and make you feel you are at peace with the world. Green has many beneficial effects on the body, including relieving nervous tension, helping to reduce headaches and neuralgia, fighting infection, and soothing digestive upsets. Could green's soothing and balancing qualities be one of the reasons it is used so often in hospital color schemes?

BLUE. This is the great healing color, so it is especially important to tune into blue's healing energies whenever you are feeling ill, run down, or in need of rest. Blue will soothe you, stimulate your body's immune system into action, and help keep you calm and relaxed. It also has powerful antiseptic qualities, which you can use in many ways. If you've got a sore throat, wrapping a blue scarf around your neck will help to reduce pain and inflammation, and you can speed up your skin's recovery from a burn, scald, sting, or bruise by placing a clean piece of blue cloth over the affected area. In fact, blue has such marvelous healing energies that I can't understand why bandages aren't made in this color!

If you find it hard to relax and go to sleep at night, choose blue bedclothes and bed linen. Keep a soothing picture in a blue frame by your bedside, or decorate your bedroom in a soft shade of blue. Put on blue clothes before you meditate because they will help to lull you into relaxation and the right frame of mind.

INDIGO. If you need to conquer fear or anxiety, this is the color to concentrate on. It is the color of intuitive insight, has a powerful effect on the mind, helps you boost your psychic abilities, and is good at lifting depression and relieving mental disorders. Indigo stimulates the subconscious—the source of some of our most creative ideas. Use it too for problems that affect the bones, such as rheumatism, and disorders of the skin and blood, such as varicose veins, ulcers, and boils. Like blue, indigo is excellent if you suffer from insomnia, so choose pillowcases in deep blue colors if you find it hard to unwind and go to sleep at night. You might find your dreams to be more intense than usual, however!

VIOLET. This is the most spiritual color in the spectrum, and it is also highly creative. In fact, if you want to boost your spiritual energy, and inspiration, you should surround yourself with violet objects or work in a predominantly violet room. Be careful, however, because violet has such a powerful effect that it can make some people feel ill or frustrated. It should also be avoided if you are feeling depressed—focus on green and blue instead.

As well as helping your inspiration flow, violet also helps boost your self-confidence, although it does so in a much more subtle way than red. Violet is a good color for people who find it difficult to love or respect themselves, or who suffer from feeling inferior and second-rate. It also helps to heal nervous complaints and scalp disorders that are sparked off by nerves.

Living with Color

I have outlined some of the ways you can benefit from the different colors in your life. You should also know that the colors you wear say a great deal about you because they reflect the real you. Open your closet now and look at the different colors of your clothes. Does one color predominate? Are there some clothes that you've rarely worn because you just don't feel good in them? Let's pretend that most of your clothes are black. Now, you might say that black goes with everything and it's always in fashion, which is true. But how do you feel when you're wearing it? Do you feel elegant and sophisticated, or do you feel slightly listless, tired, and unadventurous? And how do people react to you when you're wearing black? Do they react in a different way when you're in red or blue? Black can have a very draining effect on the emotions, especially if it's the only color you wear. So please, next time you slip into your favorite all-black outfit, put on some underwear in a color that will help to combat the depressing tendencies of black. It will make a big difference in the way you feel. Brown is another difficult color to wear because it can also make you feel gloomy and may make you seem quite drab to others. Think carefully about what the colors of your clothes say about you, especially when you are deciding what to wear to a job interview, romantic date, or important meeting.

Another significant way that color affects you is in your home. Do you have a favorite room in your home? And do you know why it's your favorite? Could it have something to do with the colors it's decorated in? Color can make a room feel warm or chilly—reds and pinks make you feel warm and cosy while pale and icy blues have the opposite effect. That's why many interior designers choose warm reds and pinks for rooms that don't get much sun, and decorate very hot and sunny rooms in cool blues and greens. If you don't like one of your rooms very much, changing the colors in it could make all the difference. Even if you don't want to redecorate the whole room you could hang up a painting that's full of the colors you like best, change the colors of the curtains, or add some big cushions in your favorite color.

You also need to think carefully about the colors you use for particular rooms in the house. Bedrooms with too much red or orange in them will make you feel so energized and alive that you'll find it hard to go to sleep at night—blues and pale violets are a much better choice, especially if you suffer from insomnia or have problems relaxing. Use reds and oranges in living rooms, but keep red to a minimum in dining rooms because it can have an adverse effect on your digestion. Yellow is great for studies and orange is wonderful for kitchens unless you eat as well as cook in them. Blues and greens are good choices for bathrooms, although you should try to choose warm shades of these colors or you'll always feel cold when you're in there.

My descriptions of the way the colors of the spectrum affect us are only guidelines. If the colors affect you in different ways, that's how you should use them. We are all different, so there is no reason why what works for you should always work for other people too. You may even find that your color preferences change with time as your mind becomes more highly tuned to the subtle influences that the different colors have. Once you start working with color, you will learn that it is one of the most powerful ways of activating the mind's power there is.

CRYSTALS

～

D id you know that we're surrounded by crystals? I'm writing this book on a personal computer activated by tiny silicon chips that are all crystals. My telephone wouldn't work without the crystals it contains. The refrigerator and freezer in my kitchen would be useless without the crystals that keep them operating.

Of course, these crystals are not the type I want to talk about in this chapter. The crystals that concern us here are the precious and semiprecious gemstones and minerals that we are all familiar with, such as quartz crystal, amethyst, turquoise, malachite, carnelian, agate, diamond, sapphire, and ruby. They are all endowed with special powers and energy that can help us in our everyday lives. Later on in this chapter, I describe the extraordinary powers of some of the more popular crystals and talk about the specially energized quartz crystal that comes with this kit. First I want to tell you what crystals mean to me.

The Importance of Crystals in My Life

Some people have good-luck charms that they wear all the time, but there's no way I could wear my talisman—it must weigh about 110 pounds! It's a huge piece of quartz crystal that I bought in the early 1970s from the Brazilian branch of the H. Stern jewelry stores. Brazil is renowned for its precious and semiprecious stones, and when I traveled there H. Stern was virtually the first place I visited when I stepped off the plane. Whenever I have to travel for long periods, that piece of quartz crystal goes with me. When I am at home at my house in England, the crystal sits by the fireplace in the living room.

Long before the craze for crystals swept America and the rest of the world, I was interested in crystals. I even wrote a novel, called *Shawn*, in which the hero is an extraterrestrial who comes from a crystal planet. I knew that crystals have amazing powers, which include protection and healing, although it wasn't until 1986 that I discovered for myself just how extraordinary crystals can be.

One of my hobbies used to be buying beautiful and unique objects from the British auctioneers Christie's, and they always sent me their catalogues when they were selling the contents of houses and big estates. One day I was idly flipping through a new catalogue when my attention was riveted by a black and white photograph of a piece of crystal mounted on a pedestal. When I looked at the measurements, I thought Christie's must have made a mistake—according to them, the crystal was about 26 inches tall and 9 inches wide. I couldn't believe it was really that big, so I called them up and asked them to check the measurements. No, they assured me, there was no mistake—the crystal really was that big.

Well, I knew I had to have that crystal! It wasn't only because it was so large—some inner voice, some inner feeling, kept telling me, "You've got to have that crystal." I thought it would be interesting to know something about the previous owner of the crystal, so I had another look at the catalogue. The house that was being cleared had belonged to the English painter and aristocrat Stephen Tennent. He was an eccentric who spent a lot of his life entertaining his friends from the comfort of his bed.

CRYSTALS

I was up early on the day of the auction, so anxious that I arrived a full hour before the sale started. All the auction lots were neatly arranged and numbered, but I barely looked at them as I made my way impatiently toward the crystal that I so longed to buy. It was even more imposing than it had looked in the photograph. The moment I touched it I felt an immense vibration and energy coming from it. It was fantastic, but what if someone else wanted it and bid an astounding amount of money that I wouldn't be able to match? But the bidding was with me; when the gavel went down, I was the new owner of the crystal. When I brought the crystal home I placed it in the entrance hall, to the left of the front door. It looked very impressive and striking, standing on the black and white marble tiles of our hall.

Shortly afterward, I celebrated my fortieth birthday and threw a big party. We invited lots of friends to help me celebrate, or commiserate, depending on your point of view. During the party, my son, Daniel, who was very young then, was fooling around and climbed the stairs to the landing. Apparently he then managed to climb up the banisters and stand on the rail, where he lost his balance. We were all in the living room, laughing and talking and drinking, when we suddenly heard a thud. Immediately, I knew something terrible had happened. Everyone ran out into the hall, and there was Daniel lying in a pool of blood on the marble floor. Miraculously, he had survived the fall. We called an ambulance, and when he got to the hospital he was given something like twenty-five stitches in his chin and his lips.

The following day, I wandered into the hall from the back door. It was a very dark and dreary December morning, which matched my mood perfectly, given Daniel's accident. I glanced over at the crystal—it was almost calling me. Suddenly I saw a beam of light shoot out of it and hit the wall by the stairs, where it broke up into thousands of tiny prisms. The whole entrance hall was shining with light. It was like being in a science fiction film, and for a moment I thought I was dreaming. The light show stopped after about ten or fifteen seconds. I realized that when Daniel had fallen, the crystal had protected him in some way I can't explain. Daniel might have been much more badly injured had the crystal not been there.

After that, I made sure that every room in the house was filled with all kinds of crystals. Bowls of little quartz chips, saucers of tiny carnelian nuggets, large polished slices of malachite, boxes made from onyx, tiny crystal pyramids, and a huge amethyst geode—we have crystals everywhere, and I believe they give us an enormous amount of protection.

How to Use the Crystal in This Kit

When I first started talking to my publishers about writing this book, I was very keen to include a crystal with the kit, because I wanted to share my interest in crystals with you. The crystal in this kit can help you conquer stress, heal minor ailments, and make you feel more optimistic. Pick it up now and hold it in your hand. Look at it closely, hold it up to the light, touch its different surfaces, feel it. Close your eyes and see if any impressions come to you.

This crystal is a clear form of quartz. If you decide to learn more about crystals, you will discover there are many different kinds, in every color of the rainbow. You may fall in love with the complex green patterns of malachite, the pinky translucence of rose quartz, or the iridescent blues and greens of opal, but quartz crystal is the ideal stone to begin to learn about crystals with. It promotes wisdom, health, and a sense of emotional peace, it has strong all-around healing qualities, and it makes a good talisman and aid to meditation. There are some wonderful legends associated with rock crystal—the ancient Greeks thought it was holy water frozen by their gods on Mount Olympus, while the Japanese believed it to be the frozen breath of their sacred dragons. Another tale is that the long-lost civilization of Atlantis was very advanced because they had learned to harness the power of crystals.

Each crystal and gemstone has its own special qualities, such as inspiring courage or fostering a sense of peace, and all of them can be employed for healing, although some have specific uses. There really aren't any rules about using crystals—you have to find your own way of working with them. Some people like to wear a favorite crystal on a chain or ribbon around their necks, others like to wrap it in a little piece of silk to protect it and keep it in their pocket, while some people like to keep their crystal on their desk or by their bed. You can do any of these things with your crystal, and it will still release its protective and healing energies. When you want to meditate, you can keep staring at your crystal until that is the only thing you are aware of, or you can concentrate on the flashes of light it throws off when sunlight hits it. You could also turn yours into a pendulum (see page 104 for more details).

What to Look for When Buying a Crystal

Many specialty stores now sell crystals and semiprecious gemstones, and wandering around in them is like looking at treasures taken from Aladdin's cave. It is fascinating to think they have all been mined from the earth and that they come from all over the world. They vary a great deal in price because some are much rarer than others, but even if you are on a tight budget you should be able to find a crystal that suits you.

If you've never been in a crystal shop before, you may wonder where to start. I've given you a list of the crystals and gemstones and their traditional associations and you can choose one from this (see page 93), or you can choose a crystal that helps alleviate a particular ailment. Alternatively, you can just choose the crystals that you like. In fact, I believe we are automatically drawn toward crystals that are good for us, so follow your instincts and choose the crystals that seem right, but make sure you handle them before buying—it's very important to hold a crystal in your hand and see how it makes you feel. You might suddenly be overcome by unhappiness or depression, or develop a headache, in which case it's not the crystal for you. Put it back where you found it and look for something else. Sometimes you know that a certain crystal is the right one for you because it feels warm, or it tumbles into your hand, or you can feel the energy coming out of it. Hold it up to the light and study its clarity. Maybe you can see patterns in it, or beams of light flashing off it. Choosing a crystal is a very personal business, so be guided by your instincts and choose what *you* like, not what a friend or the salesman tells you to like!

Many books tell you to clean your crystal when you get it home, although I have to admit that I never bother. However, please don't clean the crystal that comes with this kit, or you might remove the energy I have given to it. If they are grubby or sticky, most crystals and semiprecious gemstones can be washed under cool running water or gently cleaned in lukewarm water to which you have added a drop of detergent. However, a few crystals will disintegrate when washed in this way because they consist mainly of soluble minerals, so when you buy the stone always ask if it can be washed. If in doubt, dust it with a very fine paintbrush instead. Please be careful when handling crystals and gemstones. Although they may look sturdy, some scratch very easily—amber and malachite are both soft and so are easily damaged. They also lose their sheen when worn next to the skin, as do turquoise and hematite, so wear them over your clothes.

Occasionally you may feel that you want to clean the crystals you buy in a more esoteric way. This is particularly valuable if you suspect that the crystal was handled a lot before you bought it, and you want to clear it of anyone else's vibrations. To do this, choose a quiet time and sit with the crystal on a table in front of you. Make sure that both your feet are placed on the floor, so your energy can flow easily, then close your eyes and imagine that your crystal is being washed in a beautiful stream of cool mountain water. Imagine any negative vibrations that it's picked up being washed away, leaving it clean and ready for your use. Really believe that this is true. Then open your eyes. The crystal is now clean of all negative vibrations.

Using Crystals for Healing

Now I want to tell you how crystals and gemstones can help improve your mind's ability to enhance your health and well-being, both physically and mentally. If you are worried about any aspect of your health, do get a medical checkup, and then you can use the crystal in conjunction with any medication your doctor prescribes.

CRYSTALS

Crystals and gemstones have always been prized for their beauty and shape, and also for their healing qualities. To many people, the idea that crystals can be used for healing is a weird New Age notion, but actually there's nothing new about it at all. As far back as the Stone Age, various crystals were believed to have power, and they have been credited with fantastic qualities ever since. For instance, the ancient Chinese believed that jade could give life, so they thought it could also preserve their dead, and the corpses of important people were wrapped in suits made from pieces of jade. In the past, it was quite commonplace to use quartz crystals and other stones for healing ceremonies and to ward off the evil eye—Alexander the Great made sure that each of his soldiers carried a piece of magnetite, known as a lodestone, as protection against evil spirits. Buddha used turquoise when he wanted to invoke spiritual powers that would help him fight negative entities.

I have a collection of crystals that hang above my exercise bike, and I am convinced that they give me power and energy. I think of them as crystal charms, and they have been given to me by friends from all over the world. When I feel really drained, I move a particular crystal so it hangs directly above my head. Then I can benefit from the power it emanates.

The piece of rock crystal in this kit is a good all-arounder suitable for many purposes and for healing all kinds of ailments. You can use it in various ways: You can carry it in your pocket on days when you don't feel well, you can wear it all the time to boost your energy level and ward off infection, or you can hold it in your hand and concentrate on it whenever you feel ill or lacking in energy (it is especially powerful when used in this way). Alternatively, you can simply keep it by your bedside, on a table by your favorite chair, or on your desk. The wonderful thing about crystals is that they release their energies whatever you do with them, so you can be sure that your crystal will send you healing energies whenever you need them. You don't have to wave them around or conduct strange, esoteric ceremonies with them—all you need to do is keep them near you.

Another way of using crystals and gemstones is to wear them as jewelry; I have just created my own line of crystal jewelry. You can buy some beautiful rings, bracelets, and necklaces containing crystals, and they are just as effective as a piece of unpolished crystal. In fact, you may already be wearing some powerful stones without realizing it—precious gemstones such as diamonds, sapphires, rubies, and emeralds all have healing powers, although synthetic forms of these stones do not.

There is a huge range of different crystals and gemstones with healing powers—far too many to list here, in fact—but in the following pages I describe twenty-two of the most popular and readily available crystals and stones. At the end of each description I mention which chakra is linked to the stone.

Crystals and the Chakras

Chakras are subtle energy centers within and emanating from the body. For those who can see them, chakras appear to look like spinning vortices of energy containing colors. The chakras are related to the endocrine system. Think of the chakras as centers through which energy is distributed through the body. If you wish to affect the body or its energy, including the body's aura, work with the chakras. Auras are only visible to powerful healers and mystics, who describe an aura as a luminous oval of various colors surrounding our bodies.

Here are brief descriptions of the seven main chakras of the body, telling you where they are and the functions and organs of the body that they influence.

THE CROWN. The highest of the chakras, found on the top of the head. It is linked to the central nervous system and the right eye. It is associated with our ability to worship God and be connected to the cosmos.

THE BROW. Located between the eyebrows, this chakra is associated with the pineal and pituitary glands, nose, ears, and left eye. This chakra is known as the "third eye," since it is the seat of our psychic ability.

THE THROAT. This chakra is found at the base of the throat. It is connected with speech, communication, knowledge, and truth, and affects the thyroid gland, mouth, and throat. It represents our ability to express our will.

THE HEART. Located in the center of the chest between the breasts. It is associated with unconditional love and affects the heart, circulation, blood, and lungs. It is the place of consciousness and is an important location of energy synthesis.

THE SOLAR PLEXUS. This chakra is in the center of the torso just above the navel. It is connected with the emotions and affects the stomach, liver, pancreas, and gallbladder. It is the place of our personal power and our life-preserving energy.

CRYSTALS

THE SACRAL. Found near the genitals, this chakra is connected with the emotions, sexuality, and reproduction and affects the sexual organs, adrenal glands, and bladder. Creative energy emanates from here.

THE BASE. Also known as kundalini, this chakra is located at the base of the spine. It is connected with courage and physical health and is associated with the spinal column, legs, bones, and colon. It is also the seat of our life force and affects our sheer vitality.

Besides influencing the physical processes in our bodies, chakras affect us mentally and emotionally. That's why some healers work with chakras when treating people who suffer from depression or anxiety—they believe that once they get the chakras open and spinning normally again, the patient will start to feel better because their energy will be able to flow properly once more.

If you want to work with your chakras and ensure that they are all open and spinning properly, thereby allowing your body's energy to flow freely, one way to do it is to meditate on seven different crystals, which correspond to each of the chakras (see list on pages 93–98). Each time you meditate, concentrate on a particular crystal until it fills your mind. If you want to make this visualization more powerful, you could also wear the crystal or gemstone that is linked to that chakra. Alternatively, you can meditate on whichever crystal you think of—you will automatically choose the one you need.

Placing a crystal or gemstone over the chakra to which it corresponds can have a subtle but profound effect. To do this, it is best to lie down in a quiet room at a time when you know you won't be disturbed. Relax completely. Then place the crystal or gemstone on your throat, your forehead, or whichever chakra you want to activate, and lie peacefully in that position for about thirty minutes. When you have finished, remove the crystal, gently stretch your arms and legs, and get up slowly (otherwise you may feel dizzy). If you want to place a crystal on your crown chakra, you will have to sit upright.

Important Crystals and Gemstones

Here is a list of the twenty-two crystals and gemstones that are among the most useful and easy to obtain. Though each has particular powers, the most important thing is whether you like the feel of them when you handle them. Always choose the stones you feel drawn to; they will be the ones that work best for you. If you have jewelry containing any of these stones, observe how you feel when wearing it; you might learn about the stone's effect on you.

AGATE. This stone comes in many colors, including red, blue, and moss. It instills courage, strengthens body and mind, improves circulation, and helps the colon and pancreas to work well. It is linked to the solar plexus chakra.

ALEXANDRITE. A rare and expensive but very beautiful stone. Deep green in natural light, it changes to raspberry pink in artificial light. The Russians call it the "stone of good omen," and it is highly beneficial in healing, soothing, and refreshing the nervous system, encouraging optimism and spiritual insight, and boosting confidence. It is linked to the crown chakra.

CRYSTALS

AMBER. Amber is the fossilized sap of ancient trees and is found in many shades of yellow. It is good for improving the memory, alleviating throat and chest complaints, boosting energy and courage, and helping you cope with daily struggles. It is linked to the solar plexus chakra.

AMETHYST. Amethyst is found in beautiful purple colors and strengthens the immune system and cleanses the blood. It helps to counter anxiety and increases the intellect and intuition. It is a good stone for meditation and is linked to the crown chakra.

AQUAMARINE. Aquamarine comes in many shades of blue. It is good for purifying and balancing the emotions, and also for strengthening the kidneys, liver, spleen, and thyroid. It is excellent for meditation as it promotes tranquillity and a deep sense of calm. It is linked to the throat chakra.

CARNELIAN. This is the orange-red form of chalcedony. A good energizer and excellent for cleaning the blood and purifying the system, carnelian also helps to connect the inner and outer selves and reduces anxiety. It is great for meditation, positive thinking, and visualization, and its powers are boosted when it is combined with amethyst. It is linked to the sacral chakra.

DIAMOND. A beautiful precious stone. It is most commonly known as colorless, but some rare diamonds are pink, yellow, blue, and green. A marvelous stone for healing, it dispels negativity, purifies the body, and increases spiritual awareness. It is linked to all the chakras.

EMERALD. This stunning green precious stone is very soothing, good at combating nervous tension, high blood pressure, and eye problems. It is traditionally linked with divine forces and is therefore excellent at promoting spiritual growth through meditation. It is linked to the heart chakra.

GARNET. The color of this stone varies from almost black to green, pink, orange, and red. Use it to treat arthritis, emotional problems, and depression. It is a good talisman. Garnet is linked to the base chakra.

JADE. Jade is found in different shades of green and in white. It is excellent for high blood pressure, circulation problems, diabetes, kidney diseases, and heart trouble; mentally, it encourages serenity, love, wisdom, and modesty. It is linked to the solar plexus chakra.

JASPER. Jasper ranges through many colors, from yellows to greens, blues, and reds. A powerful healing stone that is good for the whole body, it is especially effective in treating problems with the liver, gallbladder, and bladder, and in curing emotional problems and heartache. It is linked to all the chakras.

LAPIS LAZULI. A stone that is found in beautiful shades of blue, lapis lazuli is excellent at boosting psychic abilities and helping in spiritual development. It is a powerful healer, particularly good for digestive problems, epilepsy, brittle bones, and thyroid problems. Don't wear it for too long because it can divorce you from reality. It is linked to the brow and throat chakras.

MALACHITE. Malachite is marked with fascinating green bands of color. A powerful healer, it is particularly useful for combating insomnia, improving the circulation, and helping the spleen and pancreas to work properly. It is good at balancing the emotions and excellent at aiding visualization. It is linked to the solar plexus chakra.

MOONSTONE. A colorless stone with a blue or silvery sheen to it, moonstone balances the emotions, helps with mental disorders, improves logic and intuition, and dispels water retention. It is a very feminine stone and has been traditionally linked with fertility. Moonstone is linked to the heart chakra.

OPAL. A multicolored stone with a beautiful iridescent quality, opal invigorates, boosts creativity, improves eyesight, and enhances intuition and spiritual insight. It is linked to the brow chakra.

QUARTZ CRYSTAL. The crystal that comes with this kit, quartz crystal is excellent at combating negative thinking and negative energy forces. It is very good at boosting energy, positive thoughts, and intuition, and encourages wisdom and emotional peace. A good all-arounder, it is linked to all the chakras.

ROSE QUARTZ. Rose quartz is found in lovely soft shades of pink and gray. It is very good at combating fear, anxiety, stress, and negative emotions and helps to release anger, jealousy, and guilt. As it boosts the imagination and the higher mind, it is a good choice for meditation. It is linked to the heart chakra.

RUBY. This beautiful red precious stone is excellent for healing blood disorders (a Hindu legend says that rubies are diamonds mixed with blood) and liver problems and for boosting the immune system. It creates emotional balance, promotes integrity, optimism, and a sense of calm, and combats jealousy. It is linked to the heart chakra.

SAPPHIRE. The best-known form is dark blue, but sapphires are also occasionally found in pale blue, pinky-violet, orange, yellow, and green. This stone is very good at combating fevers, nervous ailments, and asthma, and it creates a sense of spirituality and peace. It is linked to the brow chakra.

TOPAZ. The colors of this stone vary from smoky yellows and toffees to blues. Topaz is an excellent detoxifier and is good at healing throat problems, coughs, and nerve-related ailments, including skin problems. It has a soothing quality and fosters wisdom and self-expression. It is linked to the brow chakra.

TOURMALINE. The beautiful tourmaline has more colors than any other gemstone, including yellow, green, blue, pink, and red. It has a protective influence, galvanizes self-confidence, and dispels fear. It is particularly effective for mental imbalances and disorders, boosting willpower, and creating an emotional balance; it also helps indigestion, excessive gains and losses of weight, throat problems, and gout. It is linked to all the chakras.

TURQUOISE. This stone has given its name to its blue-green color. A wonderful healer that boosts the body's system, it helps tissue to regenerate and protects against environmental pollutants. It enhances love, friendship, loyalty, communication, and creative self-expression. It is linked to the throat chakra. Stones that are merely dyed turquoise do not possess its healing qualities.

You can use any of the twenty-two stones in this section on crystals and gemstones in the ways I've already described, such as wearing a particular one as a piece of jewelry or keeping it by your bedside. For example, Alexandrite is particularly powerful and will bring you most benefit if you wear it all the time. Or you can collect a library of crystals and stones that you use for specific purposes. Rose quartz is very effective in promoting a peaceful, harmonious atmosphere, so it's a good crystal to keep around the house, especially in all the rooms you use the most. Women who suffer from premenstrual tension will benefit if they wear a moonstone during the two weeks leading up to their monthly period, because it helps to reduce water retention. Next time you have a bad cough or suffer from a chest cold, hold a piece of topaz in each hand whenever you're relaxing or resting, and tell yourself that the crystal will help to speed up your recovery.

DOWSING

~~~

In dowsing, a physical object is used to indicate the presence of water, minerals, and other objects. I have done an enormous amount of dowsing, but I don't use special metal rods, forked twigs, or pendulums, all of which are the traditional dowser's tools—I use my hands.

Over the years, several major companies have commissioned me to dowse for oil and minerals. Private individuals and police forces have asked me to use my dowsing powers to help them find missing persons and kidnap victims. Each time I use the same technique, whatever I am looking for. It may seem strange that dowsing should work equally well whether you are looking for a seam of gold or a lost child, but it does. What's more, it seems that the dowser's skills are selective—if you are dowsing for water, you won't pick up signals from minerals, and if you are dowsing for minerals, you won't pick up signals from water.

Many people are natural dowsers, but they may not know it. Dowsing is a fascinating technique that is an extension of our sixth sense, our psychic ability. It enhances people's lives because it enables them to tune into this sixth sense and develop a sensitivity to their surroundings that they never knew they had. It's also invaluable in practical ways, such as finding sources of underground water or locating objects that have been lost outdoors.

I dowse in two stages. First, I work with a map of the area I have been asked to search, in a procedure that can take up to one hour.

Very methodically, I move my hands in straight lines about six inches above the map until I feel a strong magnetic pull on the palms of my hands. Sometimes I feel a magnetic resistance instead, as if my hand is being rejected by a magnetic force. Either sensation tells me that I have found the right area. Then I narrow down the search by pointing my finger at the area I have just selected and moving it above the map until I feel that magnetic pull again. When I do, I know that's the spot I've been looking for. It is now time for the second stage of my dowsing, when I fly in a helicopter or airplane over the area I have pinpointed and dowse it with my hands. All I do is stretch out my hands, and when I feel that magnetic pull again I tell the pilot, who marks the place on his map. Then, to confirm my findings, I get out my own map and dowse it again with my hands. If all three findings are the same, then I am almost sure that I've found the right location. One of the companies that hired me to do this work told me I had shortened the odds of finding a mineral-rich site from about three hundred to one to about three to one. As you can imagine, that saves them an enormous amount of money and time.

How Dowsing Works

As you may have seen, a dowser walks along holding a forked twig or metal rods or pendulum in his or her hands. The forked twig will jerk upward or downward when the object he or she is looking for is found, while a pair of L-shaped metal rods will cross over each other. The pendulum, which in its simplest form is a bobbin on a string held between your thumb and forefinger, works in the same way—it starts to swing in a particular way when the dowser walks over what he or she is looking for.

DOWSING

By the way, dowsing has nothing to do with witchcraft, sorcery, or black magic—there's nothing sinister about it at all. In fact, some of the most respectable companies you can think of employ dowsers. Farmers may hire dowsers to locate a hidden stream so they can use it to irrigate their land. Many water companies employ dowsers to help them trace the source of a flood, find an artesian well, or plot the course of an underground river. A dowser is simply someone who is able to tap into the natural psychic abilities of his or her own mind, and a dowser's tools act as "antennae" for that psychic ability.

How to Dowse

Many, many people can dowse, because everyone is psychic, so why not try it if you've never tried it before? All you need is a piece of simple equipment, whether it is a forked twig or a pair of L-shaped metal rods. Look for a suitable twig in your garden or nearby woods, choosing one that has grown into the shape of a Y. The forks need to be long enough for you to hold them comfortably and must be trimmed so they are of equal length. Cut off the bottom of the twig so you have a V-shape, and trim off any side growths so the two handles of your twig are smooth. If you want to make some L-shaped metal rods, the easiest way to do it is with two metal coat hangers. With a pair of pliers, cut off the neck of one coat hanger and then cut off one of its arms so you are left with a long piece with a bend in the middle. Pull on the metal until the bend becomes a right angle, and you have your first dowsing rod. Do the same with the other coat hanger, and you've got your other dowsing rod (see page 103). Now you're ready to go!

DOWSING

If, like me, you have very sensitive hands, you may not need any special equipment to dowse. That's because it's your hands that pick up the energy vibrations from whatever it is you are looking for—the forked twig, set of metal rods, or pendulum simply amplifies those tiny vibrations so you can actually see that you are getting a response. It's your *body* that's the real piece of dowsing equipment.

The rest is up to you. If you have a garden, you can use your new equipment to dowse for an underground stream. Hold the two ends of the forked twig horizontally at waist height, or hold a metal rod in each hand at waist height with the rods sticking straight out in front of you. Now walk around slowly and concentrate on what it is you are looking for. Use some of my techniques from chapter 1 to visualize that object: Use your willpower and tell yourself, "I KNOW where it is." Your twig will start to twitch or your rods will start to cross. If you're not getting anything, don't give up. Try dowsing somewhere that you know has lots of water—walk along a riverbank or across a bridge that spans a river, and see what sort of reaction you get from your dowsing equipment. If you are a dowser, your wrists will twitch involuntarily and your forked twig will shoot up or down, and your metal rods will cross. Success will come with practice, concentration, visualization, and willpower.

Using a Pendulum

A pendulum will help you to look for all kinds of things. It, too, is a tool to tap into your psychic ability. You can use it like a dowsing tool to detect the presence of water, minerals, energy fields, or archaeological sites, as well as to locate missing objects or people.

USING METAL L-RODS

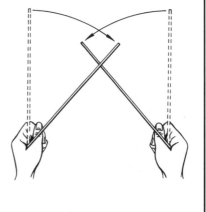

L-rods can be made by cutting two coat hangers as shown here. Make two Ls by bending the wire out to a right angle.

To begin, hold the rods straight out in front of you. The L-rods will cross to indicate that you are over a target.

Whatever you use it for, the way in which the pendulum swings will tell you whether or not you have found what it is you are searching for.

But that's not all a pendulum can do—it will also answer questions with a "yes" or "no" response according to the direction in which it swings. These answers don't come out of thin air or from some higher source—they actually come from *you*. How? I believe that when you ask a question, minute vibrations in your fingers are transmitted down the cord or string from which the pendulum is suspended and affect its orbit. Even though your conscious mind may not know the answer to the question you are asking, your subconscious mind does. The pendulum is a tool of your mind. And if that sounds incredible, remember that this book is full of examples of how you can train your mind to produce all sorts of fantastic feats. Many different objects make suitable pendulums—all you need is something heavy enough to swing well and with a hole through which you can thread a piece of cord, ribbon, or chain. As a general rule, the heavier the pendulum, the longer this cord or chain should be in order to allow it to swing properly. You may already have a pendant or medallion you can use, or you can buy a pendulum that has been specially made for the purpose. Choose one that you like and that feels good when you swing it around. This is a very personal choice, so take your time making up your mind.

If you prefer, you can use the crystal that comes with this kit as a pendulum. Wrap a piece of wire around the top edge of the crystal (faceted point down) and then give it an "eye" or jump ring over the top. Thread a chain or piece of cord through the jump ring and hold it at different lengths until you find one that feels right and allows the pendulum plenty of movement. Gather up the excess chain or cord in your hand so it doesn't get in the way of the pendulum's swing.

Asking the Right Questions

The pendulum produces "yes" and "no" answers according to the direction in which it swings when you ask it a question. Before you start to use your pendulum you must first make sure that you have established exactly what these directions are, because different pendulums have different ways of answering—swinging backward and forward may mean "yes" and swinging from side to side may mean "no," or vice versa, or your pendulum may have two completely different swings. The first thing to do is to check how your pendulum swings. You can do this in two ways. The first is by asking it some very simple questions to which you already know the answers, and which can only be answered with a "yes" or "no." For example, test the pendulum's responses by holding it over a wooden tabletop and ask, "Is this table made from wood?" Keep your hand still and watch the movement of the pendulum. After a couple of seconds the direction of its swing will start to change. Wait until it settles into a definite direction, such as backward and forward or side to side. Remember what that direction is, then ask the question again and see if the pendulum reacts in the same way. If it does, that means you know what its response for "yes" is. Now you've got to find out what "no" is, so hold it over your leg, or a piece of carpet, and ask the question, "Is this leg/carpet made from wood?" Then see which movement it settles into. It should be very different from the "yes" answer. If it isn't, try again and see if you get a "no." If you still aren't having any luck, try the pendulum with a different object and again ask a straightforward question to which the answer can only be "no."

Another way to discover the pendulum's "yes" and "no" swings is to ask it to show them to you. You can do this aloud or in your head. Hold the pendulum's cord loosely between your thumb and forefinger and ask, "Show me your 'yes' response." Make a note of the pendulum's motion. Then ask, "Show me your 'no' response," and make a note of that, too. Do this several times until you are absolutely sure of what is "yes" and what is "no." If you like, you can also ask your pendulum to show you its "don't know" response. You'll get this when you've asked the pendulum something it can't answer, usually because you haven't phrased the question properly.

By the way, sometimes the pendulum will alter the direction of its "yes" and "no" answers, so check these every time you start to use it. It takes only a couple of minutes and will ensure that you and the pendulum understand each other and that it gives you the correct answers.

Remember that the pendulum is just a tool for your psychic ability. It responds to the power of your mind. You need to practice using it not only so that you and it can get used to each other but also to practice your psychic ability. Don't be disappointed if you get some wrong answers at first; that's perfectly normal. Spend some time every day testing your pendulum by asking it simple questions until your rate of accuracy goes from mediocre to infallible. You can invent all sorts of simple tests, but here's one to start you off. Choose six playing cards, all numbered between two and ten, and one face card. Shuffle them well, then deal them facedown on the table in front of you. Now hold the pendulum over each card in turn and ask it if this is the face card. When it says "yes," turn the card over to see if the pendulum got it right or not. Do this again and again until your pendulum finds the face card every time.

You can do the same sort of experiment with three identical pieces of cardboard. Number each piece clearly from one to three, then turn them over and shuffle them around. Hold the pendulum over each piece in turn and ask it if this is number three. Or choose three photographs, making sure they are the same size but show different things—say, a dog, a cat, and a boat. Turn them facedown, move them around, then ask the pendulum to find the photograph of the dog.

Have you got the idea? Keep on testing the pendulum until you can rely completely on its answers. You need to build up a good working relationship with your pendulum. It may take some time, but I promise that the results will be worth it. Remember, the pendulum is a tool of your mind, so train it to work in harmony with your mind until you can really trust it.

Working with the Pendulum

Once you get the hang of it—literally!—you can ask your pendulum for advice on almost everything under the sun. But remember that it can only reply "yes" and "no," so you must be careful when phrasing your questions. The more specific your question, the more accurate the answer will be. Instead of asking a rather vague question like "Is it going to rain?" you need to ask, "Is it going to rain on my house in the coming hour?" or whatever it is you want to know. There's no point asking things like "When will that package arrive?" or "Which horse will win the Derby this afternoon?" because the pendulum can't give you that sort of information. All you'll get is the "don't know" response or no response at all. But you could ask, "Will that parcel arrive tomorrow?" or "Will Boneshaker win the Derby this afternoon?"

The pendulum is especially effective when you're looking for something you've lost—you can use it to find anything from a missing cat to the break in a water pipe. Let's say you're looking for a valuable ring that you put in a safe place before you went on vacation. Unfortunately, it was such a safe place, and you were in such a hurry, that now you can't remember where it is. How are you going to find it? You can look for it the conventional way and spend days turning the house upside down, going through every drawer and cupboard in the place until you find it, or you can consult your pendulum. I know which option I'd take! This is what you do.

First of all, of course, you need to check the "yes" and "no" responses. When you've got them sorted out, you can ask your pendulum to help you look for your missing ring. You may want to keep some paper and a pen beside you so you can jot down the results or any ideas that come to you. Ask the pendulum if your missing ring (describe it to the pendulum so it knows which ring to look for) is in the kitchen. See what it says and write down the results. If the answer is "no," ask if it is in the hallway, and continue asking the questions until the pendulum says "yes." If it says "no" to each question, then check that you and the pendulum agree about what the "no" response is, and also check that you are asking a simple, straightforward question. Rephrasing the question may give you better results.

Once the pendulum has told you which room the missing ring is in, take the pendulum into that room with you. Now you'll have to hold the pendulum over each piece of furniture in the room in turn and ask a new question—"Is my missing ring hidden in this piece of furniture?" Let's say you get a "yes" when you hold the pendulum over the chest of drawers. Narrow down the search by pointing to each drawer in turn with one hand while holding the pendulum in the other. Ask, "Is my missing ring hidden in this drawer?" When the pendulum says "yes," open up the drawer and start looking for your ring.

Use the energized crystal in this kit as a pendulum or buy a gemstone that you really like and start to practice with it. It could bring you good luck. Let the force of your mind flow and forge a deep harmony with your pendulum. Once you've learned to use it properly, I can assure you that you'll wonder how you ever managed without it!

HOW TO DEVELOP YOUR ESP

~~~~

D espite what the biology books may tell us, I believe we have six senses. Touch, taste, smell, sight, and hearing—and ESP. To me, it makes perfect sense, and perhaps ESP is the perfect sense. It cuts through time and space, triggers our intuition, brings people together, allows us to stay in touch with one another even though we may be thousands of miles apart, and can act as a warning when we're facing danger. I believe that everyone has the gift of ESP, whether they know it or not. But what is it?

ESP means extrasensory perception, and to me it means psychic ability and includes telepathy or mindreading. We all possess these powers in greater or smaller amounts, even though we may not realize it. Some people read about the talents of famous psychics and mediums and tell themselves that because they don't have the same abilities they aren't psychic. But I disagree.

Have you ever suddenly started thinking about someone you haven't heard from for a long time, and then received a letter or phone call from him or her out of the blue? Or have you ever been sitting quietly at home with a partner or friend and started to think about a particular book or film for no reason at all, only to have the other person begin to talk about it? I think experiences like these are caused by telepathy, and most of us have had them at some time in our lives. They are exciting or even remarkable but are easily forgotten. The experiences that do stick in our minds are the ones connected with a crisis, which is when ESP seems to flow particularly well. Just as you might discover running skills you never knew you had when you're chased by a rabid dog, so your most remarkable experiences with ESP might happen at a crunch point in your life.

It is difficult to explain how telepathy works because no one yet knows for certain, but I believe that our brains are like cables

TIPS FOR TUNING IN TO THE ENVIRONMENT

- When you first walk into a place you have never visited before, clear your mind of distractions and wait to see what impressions come to you. Do you sense an energy? An emotion? Does the temperature seem very warm or extra chilly?
- Alternatively, you may start to pick up on the energy of the room or place you are visiting after you have been there for some time. Wait until you are relaxed, then clear your mind and see what impressions come to you.
- Take note of any images or mental pictures that

full of wires, each with its own task to perform. There are wires for seeing, hearing, thinking, walking, and all the other activities we take for granted, and also wires for telepathy, which I think travels faster than the speed of light. In this chapter and those following I'm going to show you how to develop and strengthen your psychic ability so that you can make full use of your sixth sense. You can use it to spot parking spaces, for knowing when people are going to

spring to mind. You might suddenly think of a child, or a river, or some other person or thing that has no rational reason for entering your consciousness. Check up later to see if there is a connection. Try not to feel frustrated if you have a very clear and vivid impression of something no one can explain. It may be that you have glimpsed the future, not the past.

· Bring your eyes out of focus slightly. Can you "see" or "sense" subtle vibrations in the air? This will generally be light, but are there areas where the energy "feels" darker, or in shadow, or even lighter or more bright?

let you down, and for communicating with the people who are close to you emotionally.

I use telepathy all the time in my life, but one of the most striking examples was when I used it to make money—something I bitterly regretted afterward. It was in the mid-1970s, when I was still busy making a name for myself in America and Europe, and, although my earnings were good, I couldn't shake off the memory of growing up with not enough money. One night I went to a casino in London and started to play roulette. My luck was with me because I knew exactly where the roulette ball was going to fall each time the wheel stopped spinning. By the end of the evening, my winnings totalled $25,000, and the crupiers were eyeing me suspiciously—I think they were glad to see me go! I don't know whether my winnings that night were due to telepathy, which enabled me to predict where the ball would land, or psychokinesis, which enabled me to make the ball land where I wanted. Either way, it was a dramatic example of what the mind can do.

The following day I was being driven in a sedan along one of Britain's busiest motorways, with the money tucked safely into my inside jacket pocket. I was idly looking out of the window when I was suddenly almost deafened by an incredibly loud noise. At first I thought it was in the car, but then I realized that it was in my head. What was happening? I heard a very clear voice saying to me, "Why did you do it?" I knew there was only one thing it could be referring to—my trip to the casino the night before. I started shouting at the driver to stop the car, but the glass partition separating the front of the car from the back was too thick and he couldn't hear me. I hammered on the partition until it broke, yelling "Stop the car! Stop the car!" He slammed on the brakes, the car slowed to a halt, and the passenger doors flew open. I was lifted bodily out of the car and unceremoniously dumped facedown on the pavement. It felt as though a massive weight were pressing down on my body, and although it can only have lasted for about ten seconds it seemed like several lifetimes. Suddenly, the weight vanished and I was able to get to my feet. As I brushed the grit off my clothes and tried to catch my breath, I caught the eye of the driver, who by this time was looking panic-stricken. It was written all over his face that he thought he had a madman for a passenger. I climbed back in the car, told the driver to go on, and leaned back in my seat, feeling completely shaken. Once we were back in the flow of traffic, I pulled the wads of banknotes out of my pocket, wound down the window, and flung them into the air. I have often wondered who found the money and what they did with it. Did it bring them luck or misfortune? One thing I do know—I never tried winning at a casino again.

Telepathy is a remarkable tool, but you must use it wisely. Never be tempted to abuse or prostitute your powers as I did that day, or you will be taught a lesson, as I was.

Many secret agencies use telepathy. In the early 1970s, the CIA in America learned that the Russians were using telepathy, so they started to develop their own program of telepathic espionage at the Stanford Research Institute in California. One of the many things they did was to train suitable service personnel to become what they called "remote viewers"—people who were able to use their telepathic powers to tune into places they had never visited and to describe what they saw there. For instance, a remote viewer would be given a map reference, nothing else, and would then describe everything he saw there. Somehow, he was able to visualize the location from a string of numbers. As you can imagine, these map coordinates always referred to buildings and installations that were owned by other countries and that the CIA wanted to know more about. After a while, the researchers realized that the system worked just as well when they gave their remote viewers a string of random numbers or no numbers at all. In some extraordinary way, the viewers' brains were still able to lock onto the right location. It was like remote spying, and there was no danger involved because the telepathic spy was safely ensconced in a room in the Stanford Research Institute. It is only recently that the CIA has started to talk about this openly, and although they will not release figures showing how successful the experiment was, it must have been worth their while because it continued for over ten years.

Psychic Exercises

Telepathy and other forms of psychic ability are skills that can be developed, but it takes practice, just like learning to play the guitar. It's not something you can learn to do overnight. All you have to do is trust in your instincts and have the courage to risk getting it wrong sometimes. Shrug off your mistakes, learn from them if necessary, and start again. Even experts get it wrong sometimes. Sure, I have days when my powers are as sharp as a needle, but I also have days when they don't work properly at all. That's because people aren't machines; they have their good and bad days. Come to think of it, even some machines can have their good and bad days.

For some of these exercises, you will need willing helpers. Choose people who are open-minded and interested in developing their ESP also—forget anyone who thinks it's all a joke or who pokes fun at it, because they probably won't take it seriously enough. It's best to start your experiments with something very simple, such as guessing which playing card one of you is looking at. Give everyone a pad of paper and a pencil so that they can write down their results—that way, you've got proof of everyone's answers. Shuffle the playing cards, then choose one at random and stare hard at it. Make sure no one else can see it. Now try to beam the image you are seeing into the minds of the other people taking part in the experiment. I find the best way to do this is to use visualization and draw the image mentally, over and over again, really concentrating while I do it. Set a time limit for each attempt (otherwise you might sit there for ages), then see how everyone did. Be patient, because it can take a while for people to relax enough to allow their ESP to start working. Keep trying, and see how you do.

Once you've got the hang of numbers, you can try telepathy experiments with letters of the alphabet, names of cities, people's names, types of animal, or whatever else you choose. You can draw simple shapes and transmit their outlines into other people's minds. You can throw dice and see if your friends can tune into which number comes up. You can also choose colors, or combinations of colors, such as pink with a blue stripe running through it. It's not as difficult as it sounds, because our brains are like muscles. You know how painful it can be when you exercise a part of your body that you haven't used in a long time—well, exercising a new part of your brain can be just as difficult. But remember, just because you haven't used your telepathic abilities much in the past doesn't mean they don't exist. Once you get accustomed to using telepathy in your life, you'll find it useful in all kinds of ways.

Some people take to telepathy experiments like a duck to

water, while others have a lot more trouble. If you find it difficult to let the messages come through, maybe you're stopping yourself from succeeding. Ask yourself honestly if part of your brain is saying, "This won't work," "This is all nonsense," or "I'm no good at this." If so, you need a little encouragement. Turn to the chapter on visualization, in which I describe how to psych yourself into doing things. Visualize yourself succeeding at the telepathy experiments, and really believe it or turn to the section in the willpower chapter called "Beat Negative Thinking" and practice thinking positively. Then try again—visualization and willpower may make all the difference in your results.

How to Become More Sensitive to Your Environment

Have you ever been for a walk along a lovely stretch of countryside and suddenly experienced a sense of peace, of being completely at one with the world around you, as though you were part of the trees, the sky, the birds? It's a marvelous, intense feeling known as a peak experience. Problems fade away and life takes on a different perspective. In my chapter on visualization, I describe how to mirror yourself (see pages 18–19), which helps you to develop this sense of being at one with the world. Once you have experienced it, a lot of the ideas that I outline in this chapter will make a lot of sense to you.

The more you develop your ESP with the help of the exercises at the beginning of this chapter, the easier you'll find it to tune into the people around you. And I don't mean trying to probe their minds to discover their innermost thoughts, but learning to distinguish the times when they want to be alone, or are feeling miserable and need comfort, or when it simply isn't convenient for them to see or talk to you.

Everyone drops subconscious hints about how they feel, if you know what to look and listen for. When you are with a friend or loved one, their body language will tell you a lot about the way they are feeling. Some really good books are available on body language, but here are a few guidelines. Is the person sitting with his arms crossed, body turned away from you, legs crossed away from you, or shoulders hunched up? If so, he may be feeling nervous, defensive, angry, or hostile. Once you notice something like that, you can try to make the person feel more at ease, ask yourself if you've done something to make him angry, or make your excuses and leave. Perhaps he's just having a bad day.

You can also tell when someone is feeling receptive toward you. He may be sitting with his body turned toward you, legs crossed in your direction or arms spread outward as if he is reaching out to the whole world. These are all signs that he is feeling relaxed and expansive toward you. If you realize that you are both sitting in exactly the same pose, like mirror images of each other, that's a great sign. It shows that you are feeling at ease with one another, and if you shift your position in some way you'll probably see your companion follow suit.

It is also important to tune in to the effects that you may have on other people. We all know people who are apparently oblivious to the needs and feelings of those around them—the sort of people who are so wrapped up in themselves that they have no energy or interest left for anyone else. They are often the ones who end up alone, unable to understand why they have so few friends and why no one phones them any more. On the other hand, we all know people who go to the other extreme and who always put themselves last, who have such a poor sense of themselves that they seem to lose their personalities completely. I think you need to strike a balance between the two extremes and learn to love yourself while also respecting other people. I describe how to grow to love yourself on pages 16–18, but here I want to talk about tuning in to the way other people feel.

Many parents have an instinctive ability that tells them when their children are in trouble or unhappy. They only need to see their faces briefly or hear their voices on the telephone to know that something's wrong. Many couples who have been together for a long time have the same telepathic link. You can develop the same intuition with people you don't know very well.

A simple exercise that helps you to tune into the thoughts and feelings of other people involves noticing your first impressions when you walk into a room or meet someone. Usually, these will be feelings and sensations that you haven't experienced until that moment. Do you feel hot or cold? Are you happy, or do you sense a sudden feeling of sadness or depression? Do any of your limbs hurt, or does your back tense up? Feelings like these may be coming from the other person, so take note of them. But don't blurt out, "You must have a headache, because my forehead hurts" or "I know you're feeling sad." You must appreciate that the person you're with may not want you to reveal his private business. Instead, you may be able to work your impressions into the conversation in a subtle way later on, or ask the person how he is and see if he admits he's got an awful headache or he's feeling sad. As with all the techniques described in this book, practice makes perfect. Don't be fazed or put off if you get lots of things wrong at first. Even later on you're unlikely to be 100 percent right, because even very psychic people can get things wrong sometimes.

Tuning in to the energy in a room or a place can take a little more practice, but is an invaluable technique. If you use your six senses you will be able to feel the vibrations in the air around you. You may even be able to see the energy move around you. You will be able to tune in to the atmosphere in houses—something that's particularly useful if you're house hunting. One day, you might even be one of those lucky people who listen to their sixth sense and suddenly decide not to board a particular airplane or drive down a certain street, only to hear later that their intuition saved them from certain death.

Wouldn't the world be a better place if everyone was aware of the effect they had on their surroundings, not only physically but mentally too? Imagine walking through streets free of litter, dog mess, discarded chewing gum, and puddles of oil and gas. Of course, you can help to create a cleaner environment yourself by respecting your surroundings and making sure you don't make a mess of them, but you can also change things on a more subtle level.

I believe that nature is a living entity, part of God, and I don't think that nature is going to stand the amount of pollution on our planet much longer. In my opinion, the major recent earthquakes in Japan, Russia, and California have occurred not only because of seismological shifts in the earth's crust but also because nature is screaming for help. Our little bodies, our little minds, can help even if it's on a molecular level. If you like what you read in this book and start to put some of it into practice, you will improve yourself and your immediate environment and therefore the planet. If you help yourself and, through that, help other people, a positive energy will spread. If you don't believe me, think how fast negative energies, such as anger or hatred, can breed. Well, there's no reason why positive, loving energies can't multiply in the same way.

All these techniques will help you improve your relationships because they are improving your perception and understanding of the world. Most important of all, you need to listen to your instincts and hunches when developing your sixth sense. Some of them will turn out to be wrong, but some of them will be right, and that's a great feeling.

How to See Ghosts

This section is going to raise a few eyebrows. There are plenty of people who are firmly convinced that ghosts do not exist. On the other hand, there are plenty of people who do believe in them and who can recount stories or even produce photographs to back up their claims. If you aren't sure whether you believe in them or not, or want to know more about them, I suggest you read a few good books on the subject and then make your decision. Certainly if you've read this far in this book, you're probably fairly open-minded.

The number of people I know who'd love to see a ghost! I have to admit that I'd also love to see one but haven't as yet managed to, although I did hear one moving about in the house that belonged to my friends Robert Bolt and Sarah Miles.

What are ghosts? No one yet knows for sure, though theories are aired, but I think they are the energy left behind by human be-ings who have died but don't want to move on to the afterlife, and so their essence remains on the earth plane. It is as if their presence has been recorded on the atmosphere, like sounds being recorded on magnetic tape, and is rerun every now and then. Some ghosts are benevolent and even protective, some are mischievous, and some are just plain scary. There have been some notorious hauntings that have turned out to be nothing more than someone faking the evidence—and, in the process, casting further doubt over the existence of ghosts—but other hauntings have no simple explanation at all and seem to be the work of genuine ghosts.

How do you see a ghost? First of all, you have to awaken your psychic powers by doing the exercises in this book, and especially the ones in this chapter. The more you can tune into a place's energy (see the checklist below), the more likely you are to sense any ghostly apparitions. Secondly, you may not see a ghost if you live in a place that's never been reported as haunted, so you might prefer to visit somewhere that is known to be so, such as a historic house. Once you're there, try to open your mind to your surroundings and tune in to the atmosphere. If the place you are visiting allows photography, take as many shots as you can. All kinds of weird phenomena that couldn't be seen with the naked eye have been captured on film, from ghosts to UFOs.

Of course, ghosts don't always materialize to order, as every professional ghost hunter will tell you, so be prepared for nothing to happen. Incidentally, you may never see a ghost, but you may hear, feel, or sense it. The temperature may plummet (one theory for this is that the ghost is drawing on the surrounding energy), the electricity may flicker or fail for no apparent reason (after this happens, check the fuses, switches, and lightbulbs and also with your neighbors in case there was a general power cut), or you may see objects moving. But here's a word of warning—when you're on a ghost-hunting mission, don't automatically assume that any odd noises you hear, or sudden drafts, are caused by a ghost. You have to rule out every other possibility before you can begin to suspect that you've experienced paranormal activity. Some hot water pipes can sound really strange when they're warming up or cooling down, especially if you've never heard them in action before. Trees rustling in the wind can sound just like a woman's long dress rustling when she walks, and when old wooden furniture relaxes it can sound uncomfortably like ghostly tappings!

You may be eager to see a ghost, but please don't invite one into your home by setting up a Ouija board or improvising a séance with letters of the alphabet and a wine glass. Psychically, that's the equivalent of opening your front door and inviting every passerby to come and visit, regardless of what they look or act like.

Talking to Animals

Anyone who loves animals talks to them. It's a natural response. But how many people actually believe that the animals can understand what they're saying? We've all seen a dog react when we start to talk about it. The dog's ears prick up and it often turns to watch us speaking. And have you noticed that dogs and cats don't like it if you make fun of them or laugh at them? They give you a pained look, as if they are disappointed in you, and stalk off in as dignified a way as possible.

Animals understand what we say to them. They can also tune in to our thought waves and are particularly good at telepathy. Our five dogs know when we're going away and become sad before the event. Talking to animals is a great way to practice your telepathy.

You don't have to talk to your animals out loud for them to un-derstand you. You can communicate just as well in your head. Try it—mentally ask your dog or cat to come to you. Keep issuing a simple command and see what happens. It can take a while for the animal to respond, but don't give up. I have a friend who is fond of the cat that lives next door to her mother. Whenever this friend is going to visit her mother, she sends out thought waves to the cat, who is called Pixie, telling her that she's coming home and asking Pixie to meet her at the garden gate at a particular time. And it usually works!

It's not only domestic pets who respond to thought waves. Next time you walk through a field of sheep or cows, try sending out mental messages to them, saying that you haven't come to harm them. See if they respond any differently from normal.

Talking to Plants

Some people have such green fingers that they could probably even make a wooden clothespeg sprout if they planted it in the garden. Other people can't keep a plant growing for long before it withers and dies. There may be all kinds of reasons for that, but I suspect that one of them concerns the person's attitude to plants. Plants *do* react to us. Scientists have conducted experiments on plants that indicate that they are able to recognize their owners, that they react to music, and that they enjoy being stroked. If a plant is ill-treated by someone—perhaps they pull some of its leaves off, or re-peatedly say how ugly it is—the energy field of the plant will dramatically alter the next time that person comes into the room.

If you want a plant to grow well and be happy, keep playing it gentle, soothing music and then watch it flourish.

You can try a simple experiment for yourself if you think all this sounds too farfetched for words. Buy two houseplants of the same variety, and check that they are both in good condition. Take them home, then put one in a room that you use a lot and leave the other one in a room that you rarely go into, your spare room perhaps. Chat away to the plant in the first room and ask it how it is every day (but don't overwater it or you'll kill it off). Don't speak to the plant that's all by itself in that spare room. You'll still have to water it, but do it with bad grace. Then keep an eye on both plants and see what happens. Experiments done in the past suggest that the plant you chat to will shoot up, put out lots of leaves, flower if it can, and generally look pleased with life. The neglected plant will start to look sad and won't flourish. Our effect on plants and other forms of life around us is just another example of our psychic ability, whether we know we are using it or not.

A few years ago, Prince Charles of England admitted he talked to his plants, and the furor in the media was so great that you'd have thought he'd just confessed to being Jack the Ripper and the Boston Strangler rolled into one. When the story broke I asked the two gardeners who look after my garden if they talked to their plants. "Mentally, of course," they said. "Lots of gardeners do."

PSYCHOKINESIS

You know the saying that there's nothing new under the sun? Well, there's certainly nothing new about psychokinesis, or PK for short. It is the ability to influence physical objects through the power of the mind, and the Bible is full of stories about it. For example, Lot's wife was turned into a pillar of salt; Aaron's rod became a serpent and devoured the rods of Pharaoh's magicians, which had also turned into serpents; with the parting of the Red Sea, Moses led the children of Israel out of Egypt.

Some of the world's ancient mysteries can also be explained if you believe in PK. Maybe the pyramids were built with the help of levitation, which enabled the ancient Egyptians to maneuver those heavy stones and set them in exactly the right position? Stonehenge is another piece of ancient architecture that has a big question mark hanging over it. How did those huge sarsen stones, the largest of which are estimated to weigh fifty tons each, get there? The nearest place with the same type of rock is twenty-four miles away. How was it possible for Neolithic man to balance the huge lintels on the upright stones so accurately, especially as the stones were given mortise and tenon joints to keep them in place? And how was it possible to position those huge stones so precisely that they formed a perfect astronomical calculator that still works today? People say it was done by making ramps from piles of logs, but I doubt that. I believe it was through levitation. I simply don't see how it could have been done any other way. Even today, engineers would have a hard job trying to move fifty-ton blocks of stone around.

Psychokinesis in My Life

There are two things for which I am most famous—telepathy and psychokinesis. When my powers were first publicized, people reacted as if nothing like this had ever happened before, yet in Russia scientists have been investigating PK for many years. Nina Kulagina was a Russian housewife who discovered her PK abilities quite by chance, and was able to develop them enough to move pens, matchsticks, and compass needles.

One of my most dramatic experiences of psychokinesis made headlines all over the world—twice. In 1989 I stopped Big Ben by mental power. This clock is one of Britain's most famous landmarks and is renowned for its extremely sensitive mechanism. The same thing happened when I tried the experiment again in Israel in 1994. A maintenance engineer said Big Ben had stopped because of a tight bearing in the clock movement, but I wonder . . .

How to Practice Psychokinesis

Everything in life that is worthwhile takes time, so please be patient. Psychokinetic abilities don't arrive overnight. Even if you never manage to activate your dormant psychokinetic powers, that doesn't mean they aren't there or that you're a failure. You may find instead that you're particularly good at some of the other psychic techniques described in this book.

When I teach children up to the age of seven how to bend spoons, they do it easily. Spoons, forks, keys, and other metal objects all perform perfectly for them. Do you know why? It's because they *believe* they can do it. They haven't yet learned to believe that they *can't* do it, which is how a lot of adults think. So before you start these experiments, block out all those so-called rational thoughts that say, "This is impossible."

How to Fix Broken Watches and Clocks

There aren't any warming-up exercises for PK, although the more you awaken your ESP and other powers, the more likely you are to succeed with it. First of all, you have to choose a suitable object for psychokinesis. It's good to start with a broken watch or clock, because it will be easy to see if you're having any effect on it. You can also try to mend a broken home appliance.

First of all, wind up the watch even though it is broken. Hold the watch in your hands and concentrate on it. Be very open-minded. Do not be skeptical—we're going to make this happen. On the count of three you are going to shout the word "WORK." By doing this you can activate your energy that can penetrate the broken watch. Try this exercise with me. Shout, "One, two, three, WORK!" Do this three times, and really believe in it. Now open your hand and look at the watch—is the second hand moving? Lift the watch to your ear and listen. Can you hear a tick?

Don't be discouraged if nothing happens. PK doesn't always work, especially if it's the first time you've ever tried it. I can assure you that I have days when PK won't work. If you're not having any luck, try again another day. Try it with your friends or some children, who can be particularly good at psychokinesis because they don't do it with any preconceived notions that it's impossible.

PSYCHOKINESIS

Make a big heap of all your broken watches and clocks, wind them all up, then get everyone to sit around them in a circle and concentrate. You may find that you can't activate your PK abilities when you're by yourself but that they work well when you're with other people.

If anything does occur when you do this experiment, please write to me at the address on page 132 and tell me what happened.

Using the Orange Circle

If you aren't having much luck getting your broken watches and clocks to start working again, place them on the orange circle card that comes with this kit, then do the same experiment and see if that makes a difference.

The orange circle is a very important tool, and you should use it to concentrate your powers. All you need to do is activate the dot and combine my psychic powers with yours. Place your hands on the dot for three minutes, and concentrate on all the great things you want to attract to you and your family. At the same time, look deep into my eyes in the photograph on the front cover of this kit. What should you wish for? It might be better health, it might be a new job, it might be relief from pain, or it might be selling your house. Whatever you want, concentrate completely on it for three minutes. When the time's up, put your broken appliance on the circle and see what happens.

When my orange circle was printed in the Australian magazine *New Idea* in the spring of 1993 and later appeared in the British newspapers the *Sun* and the *Daily Star*, I was inundated with letters from readers telling me about the astonishing things that had happened when they used it. Not only did broken TV sets start to work again, but spoons bent when readers held them and touched the orange circle. But don't take my word for it—try it yourself and see what happens! And don't forget to write to me if something strange or interesting happens to you.

How to Bend Silverware

Not everyone can bend metal, but you might want to try. I am going to suggest a different technique from the one I use. You should try this first, and if you can master it you can move on.

Choose an old fork or spoon. Hold the spoon or the fork loosely in your hand. Now psych yourself up by focusing all your power and energy on trying to manipulate the fork or spoon with physical strength. Feel a warmth passing through your arms into your hands. Really believe that you are altering the molecular structure of the metal and that it is going to bend. You might be amazed to find that it becomes like soft plastic in your hand and that the metal will twist. If you are successful you can try the technique that I use, which involves stroking the neck very *gently* to make it bend or melt. This is much more difficult.

Some people have dramatic success with bending silverware, while others can't do it at all. Put your silverware on the orange circle, stare at my eyes in the photo on the front cover of the kit and see if that makes a difference.

Above all, don't turn this into a competition with yourself, or you'll get so wound up that you'll actually block your powers from working. As I've already said, I have days when my powers are very weak and you'd think I'd never bent a spoon in my life!

Moving a Compass Needle

It is currently believed that when someone is practicing psychokinesis the electromagnetic field that surrounds the individual undergoes powerful changes. Maybe that explains why I can move compass needles, affect the workings of magnetometers (which are used to measure the magnitude and direction of magnetic fields), and have erased the hard disks of several computers, all in controlled conditions. There's no way I'd recommend that you start erasing the hard disk of a computer, but you could try making a compass needle move.

To do this, put the compass in front of you on a table. If you like, put it on top of the orange circle. Ideally, you need a friend with you who can watch the compass needle to see if it moves. Wait until the needle has steadied after you've put the compass on the table, then try to make the needle move. The way I do it is to close my eyes, summon all my concentration and willpower, and clench my fists together. When I can feel the energy shooting out of my eyes and forehead, I slowly move my head toward the compass needle and shout, "Move!" The compass needle usually swings around obediently. On good days, this experiment also works if all I do is shout, "Move!" at the compass. This is a good PK experiment to do with a group of friends, because I have known times when the more people who concentrate with me, the farther the compass needle moves.

PK in the Future

By now, you may be saying to yourself, "Well, this is all very interesting but what am I going to gain by teaching myself to bend

PSYCHOKINESIS

spoons?" I quite agree! Bending spoons is good fun, and I'm certainly not going to criticize it, because it helped to make me famous. I think spoon bending is important because of what it represents, not what it is. Using our psychic powers to bend spoons and forks, to mend broken watches and appliances, and to deflect the needle of a compass simply by concentrating on it is difficult; but activating our powers to change our lives for the better is much easier and a more important target to set ourselves.

LIVING WITH YOUR POWERS

~~~~~~

I f you have read this far into the book, you will know about the incredible feats our minds and bodies are capable of, and you may have tried some of them for yourself. I hope the exercises have worked well for you and that you've enjoyed experimenting with them on your own and with your family and friends.

Maybe by now you'll have started to get some exciting results from the exercises designed to boost your psychic powers. Maybe for the first time in your life you are losing weight and keeping it off, you've got a more positive image of yourself, you no longer crave cigarettes, the orange circle has helped you to fix a broken appliance, color therapy is making big changes in your life, or using a pendulum has helped you to find an object that you thought you'd lost. Maybe you're finding it easier to relax, or you've made changes in your diet that have filled you with extra energy and vitality. If you've experienced any of the above, or some strange or inexplicable events have occurred while you were doing any of the things I suggest in this kit, don't forget, I'd like to hear from you. Please write to me at this address:

Uri Geller
c/o Virgin Publishing Ltd
332 Ladbroke Grove
London W10 5AH
England

LIVING WITH YOUR POWERS

Uri can also be contacted at his web site:

http://www.urigeller.com

I am always amazed when some people say that all psychic powers can only be used for negative purposes. Of course there are such things as voodoo and black magic, and maybe they work, but I can assure you that there's nothing in this book even remotely connected with such negative and potentially evil influences. Everything that is contained in this book is *positive,* because I truly believe that our minds can work like magnets—they can attract positive and negative people, situations, and emotions. That's why people who view life from a negative standpoint will always find more things to feel miserable about—they are attracting these negative energies. What's more, even when things go well for them they will find something to complain about, or they'll moan that things could have been so much better. Some people are never happy.

On the other hand, people who look at life from a positive angle and are optimists will attract positive energies to them. Their friends and associates will share their positive attitude. It's attitude that counts, every time. You can be the richest person in the world, with the most beautiful body and the most lavish lifestyle, yet you can still have a negative attitude that makes you miserable; or you can be poor, struggling to make ends meet, fighting off illness or coping with unemployment, but you can still have a positive attitude and feel happy most of the time.

In all the chapters in this book, I have stressed over and over again that these techniques will work if you believe in them. In fact, you will be astonished at how well they can work. Willpower, visualization, psychokinesis, dowsing, and ESP are all tools of the mind, and I want you to use them in the same way that you would use any other tools that make your life easier. When you switch on the oven, you have no doubts about its ability to cook the food you are about to put in it, and you should have no doubts either about your mind's ability to bring you the results you want. They may not arrive overnight, and it may take you a while to stop letting your brain indulge in negative ideas such as "This is a waste of time," "I feel silly doing this," or "I know this won't work." If you say those sorts of things to yourself, of course things won't work—you've just programmed your mind to refuse to allow them to happen!

But if you practice the exercises in this book and really believe in them, if you practice visualization and see yourself succeeding before going for interviews, meeting your bank manager, visiting the dentist, dealing with a difficult client, or asking your boss for a raise, you will change your whole attitude to life. You will be sending out messages like "I respect myself, I believe in myself, I can do this, I am good at my job," your body language will be positive, you will speak more clearly, and people will be impressed by you. Listen to people and they will be even more impressed. Start to use the 90 percent of your brain that is lying fallow and going to waste and your life will start to open up in ways you never imagined.

The chapters explaining how to explore your untapped psychic potential will also make an incredible difference in the way you lead your life. Your intuition will be stronger, your thought processes more powerful you will find it easier to tune in to what others are thinking and feeling, and you will be in harmony with the world around you.

LIVING WITH YOUR POWERS

But let me make one thing clear. Tapping into your psychic powers will not give you negative control over others. You will be able to use telepathy to tune in to what people are thinking, perhaps even to protect you from harm or danger, but you will not be able to bend people to your will, put curses on them, or hypnotize them into doing what you want. The only person you will have power over is yourself, and if people react to you in a new way it will be because you are starting to believe in yourself and are sending out positive messages, not because you have somehow infiltrated their mental processes.

All the techniques that I describe in this book are ways of unlocking your hidden mindpower, which means they are also ways of getting to know yourself. And that is very important. If you don't know, understand, and appreciate yourself, how can you ever hope to feel that way about the people in your life? So I hope you've enjoyed reading this book and using the cassette tape, crystal, and orange circle that are contained in the kit, that they've opened your mind to all kinds of new ideas, and that you are learning to trigger the incredible powers of your mind. You have embarked on a mental journey that will bring you untold benefits and rewards and help you to view the world in a new way. I wish you health, luck, happiness, and good fortune.

HOW URI GELLER EMPOWERS *THE MINDPOWER KIT*

In order for you to achieve the maximum benefit from the tools in *The Mindpower Kit*, Uri Geller will personally empower the orange meditation circle and the crystal contained in the kit. On the first day of every month at 11:00 A.M. and 11:00 P.M. (Greenwich Mean Time), Uri will focus all his mental power on all the kits sold throughout the world to empower the circle and the crystal with positive energy. This will enhance the ability of these important tools to help you as you visualize, meditate, use your willpower, or practice any of the techniques Uri has described in this book.

The crystal and orange meditation circle will be empowered monthly by Uri, no matter what. It would always be helpful, however, if you would take a few moments at either of the times outlined above and contribute to the empowerment. You do this by first placing the crystal on the meditation circle, then closing your eyes and visualizing bright white light and positive energy surrounding the circle and entering the crystal. Reflect to yourself that this light will remain with the crystal and circle to help you in all your mindpower endeavors. If you wish, imagine Uri as he appears on the cover of this book and picture him sending his energy to you. Close the empowerment session by gently touching the circle and opening your eyes. It is especially important to do this on the first day of the first month after you buy your kit. You will now have the benefit of Uri's positive mindpower as well as your own as you use the kit to enhance your life.

For your convenience, outlined below are the equivalent times in your time zone that Uri will be performing his empowerment. Remember that it occurs on the first of every month.

Time Zone	Time Equivalent to 11:00 A.M. or 11:00 P.M. (Greenwich Mean Time)
Atlantic	7:00 A.M. or 7:00 P.M.
Eastern	6:00 A.M. or 6:00 P.M.
Central	5:00 A.M. or 5:00 P.M.
Mountain	4:00 A.M. or 4:00 P.M.
Pacific	3:00 A.M. or 3:00 P.M.
Alaskan	2:00 A.M. or 2:00 P.M.
Hawaii–Aleutian	1:00 A.M. or 1:00 P.M.